GW00372756

home

www.thegoodwebguide.co.uk

thegoodwebguide

home

debora robertson

The Good Web Guide Limited • London

First Published in Great Britain in 2001 by The Good Web Guide Limited
Broadwall House, 21 Broadwall, London, SE1 9PL

www.thegoodwebguide.co.uk

Email:feedback@thegoodwebguide.co.uk

Original series concept by Steve Bailey.

Cover photo © Ben Wood/ Yeats Design and Architecture

10 9 8 7 6 5 4 3 2 1

A catalogue record for this book is available from the British Library.

ISBN 1-903282-15-2

Project Editor Michelle Clare

Design by Myriad Creative Ltd

Printed in Italy at LEGO S.p.A.

contents

the good web guides   6

introduction   7

secure online shopping   8

user key/key to countries   9

1 decorating and DIY   11

2 soft furnishings and finishing touches   31

3 shopping   49

4 ezines and newsletters   67

5 antiques and architectural salvage   81

6 housekeeping   95

7 learning   105

8 miscellany   117

glossary of internet terms   130

index   135

how to register for free updates   143

the good web guides

The World Wide Web is a vast resource, with millions of sites on every conceivable subject. There are people who have made it their mission to surf the net: cyber-communities have grown, and people have formed relationships and even married on the net.

However, the reality for most people is that they don't have the time or inclination to surf the net for hours on end. Busy people want to use the internet for quick access to information. You don't have to spend hours on the internet looking for answers to your questions and you don't have to be an accomplished net surfer or cyber wizard to get the most out of the web. It can be a quick and useful resource if you are looking for specific information.

The Good Web Guides have been published with this in mind. To give you a head start in your search, our researchers have looked at hundreds of sites and what you will find in the Good Web Guides is a collection of reviews of the best we've found.

The Good Web Guide recommendation is impartial and all sites have been visited several times. Reviews focus on the website and what it does, rather than endorsing a company, or their product. A small but beautiful site run by a one-man band may be rated higher than an ambitious but flawed site run by a mighty organisation.

Relevance to the UK-based visitor is also given a high premium: tantalising as it is to read about purchases you can make in California, because of delivery charges, import duties and controls it may not be as useful as a local site.

Our reviewers considered a number of questions when reviewing the sites, such as: How quickly do the sites and individual pages download? Can you move around the site easily and get back to where you started, and do the links work? Is the information up to date and accurate? And is the site pleasing to the eye and easy to read? More importantly, we also asked whether the site has something distinctive to offer, whether it be entertainment, inspiration or pure information. On the basis of the answers to these questions sites are given ratings out of five. As we aim only to include sites that we feel are of serious interest, there are very few low-rated sites.

Bear in mind that the collection of reviews you see here are just a snapshot of the sites at a particular time. The process of choosing and writing about sites is rather like painting the Forth Bridge: as each section appears complete, new sites are launched and others are modified. When you've registered at the Good Web Guide site (see p.143 for further details) you can check out the reviews of new sites and updates of existing ones, or even have them emailed to you.

By registering at our site, you'll find hot links to all the sites listed, so you can just click and go without needing to type the addresses accurately into your browser.

As this is the first edition of the Good Web Guide, all our sites have been reviewed by the author and research team, but we'd like to know what you think. Contact us via the website or email feedback@thegoodwebguide.co.uk. You are welcome to recommend sites, quibble about the ratings, point out changes and inaccuracies or suggest new features to assess.

You can find us at www.thegoodwebguide.co.uk

user key

 £   Subscription

 R   Registration required

     Secure online ordering

 UK   Country of origin

introduction

Home ownership sometimes feels more like home wrangling, trying to corral the unruly beast into a safe corner, keeping on top of the maintenance, striving to keep it looking good and trying your best to stop it from running away from you. And the very tools you might use to help you out contrive to make it even more fraught and confusing. There are more books, television programmes, magazines and stores than every before whose very existence is predicated on making your home look good. Add to that the multi-headed hydra of the internet, and it's a wonder we all don't take a vow of poverty and head off to join a closed order.

When I was asked to write this book, I saw it as a wonderful opportunity to confront the confusion that having so much choice generates and turn it to our advantage. The internet could be the best decorating tool since the paint brush, if only we learn to exploit it, manipulate it and plunder it for our own stylistically-selfish ends. I hope that this book will help you to see the many home interest sites on the internet as your own personal resource, your well-stocked tool box, to help you develop your sense of style using the world wide web as your guide.

In researching this book, several things became clear very quickly. Small companies are making wonderful, creative use of the web to offer unusual, exciting products to their customers. Many of the larger companies seem to be waiting, for what it's hard to say, before they fully commit themselves to online shopping. Perhaps they just want to see if it catches on. At least one major, generally innovative, retailer has a homepage that has contained nothing more riveting than a 'Site Under Construction' logo for the past year. You'd think they were trying to build the British Library in there.

Companies that have embraced the internet are finding out that, not only are their customers becoming web-savvy, they're increasingly web-sophisticated and expect an online ordering service as just one further arm of customer service.

Of course in the world of cyber shop-keeping, things change all of the time. It is only to be hoped that the retail behemoths catch up with their younger, more sprightly brothers and sisters. If they do, you'll hear about it first by referring to our regularly updated site at www.thegoodwebguide.co.uk. In a matter of weeks, it's possible for previously exciting sites to lose their sparkle, while others improve almost beyond recognition. We will keep an eye on them so that you will be the first to know. And in the meantime, if you have any comments or suggestions, we look forward to hearing them. Have fun!

Debora Robertson, April 2001

secure online shopping

Here's the science part ...

In this security conscious age, we all worry about using our credit cards online. Fortunately, there are safeguards built into reputable ecommerce sites to allow us to shop with confidence. The most important of these is encryption technology built into our browsers (MS Internet Explorer or Netscape Navigator). The way this works is that when the website asks the browser to encrypt the data you send, using a code it provides, only the receiving website has the key to unlock your credit card details.

To check that you are using the secure site, look for a padlock in the bar at the bottom of the window. Some sites get you to enter your details on an un-secured page and then send the details via secure page, which is tantamount to giving your car keys to a complete stranger who insists he only wants to drive your BMW round the corner. This is being discouraged in the industry, as the consumer does not know if the site is secure or not until it's too late.

In some cases, web design has got ahead of the browsers, and even the most common versions of the most popular browsers do not always display the secure padlock on sites that are, indeed, secure.

This is due to a layout known as frames. When a site uses frames, the outside frame of the page often remains the same (you can see this, and the site address does not change from page to page), and the buttons that you click on, say a menu of features, change only the page in the

middle of the screen. Essentially, this is a page within a page. The effect of this is that the browser does not see that the sub-page is secure, and does not show the secure padlock symbol.

This does not mean that the page is not secure, and it is possible to check the security.

Click on the sub page (where you enter the confidential information) and then use your right mouse button (PC users), and select "Open Page in a New Frame". This will open the sub page only, in a new window, and the page will have a secure symbol on it.

Click on the sub page and then use your right mouse button (PC users), and select 'Properties'. This will show you the security information and show the address of the sub-page (it should start https// not http//). In addition the 'Connection' will show the encryption type, or display 'Not Encrypted'.

To add to the problem, some pages use a Java applet to enter and encrpt your secure details. This is a small program built into the web page which encrypts and then sends your data. As you cannot see the program details, it is not possible to check whether they are secure or not.

On the sites reviewed with Frames, all barr one (English Stamp Company) said they were moving away from Frames to ensure that their customers knew they were secure. Only one site we reviewed had a Java Applet.

decorating and DIY

Unless you were born in ill-fitting jeans with a pencil stuck behind your ear, spending the weekend shopping for DIY products makes watching paint dry look like a stimulating lifestyle choice. This is one area where online ordering really does come into its own. In many cases ordering is swift, with products sometimes arriving in less time than it takes for your enthusiasm for a project to fade. Less satisfactorily, some companies don't offer online ordering but suggest you use the web to create a shopping list you can take with you when you go to the store. If you have an image of yourself skipping merrily along the aisles picking out exactly what's on your list in less time than it takes to say 'out of stock', then you have greater faith in the DIY sheds than I do.

Of course, it's not all drill bits and two by fours. You can buy paint and paper online too, though most paint pushers quite rightly advise customers to splash around with a few sample pots before splashing out on 20 litres of what you thought was leaf green, only to find that it makes your walls look like they have a virulent outbreak of mould.

The internet provides many practical and inspirational decorating sites too. Whether you want to replace the washer on a tap or stipple your way into the pages of an interiors magazine, there is plenty to encourage and inform. If that all seems like too much hard work, there are a couple of sites that will help you with that perennial problem: finding a good trades person. Prospective plumbers and painters go through a fairly rigorous vetting procedure and their work is usually guaranteed for up to two years. Sometimes, they even help you with questions to ask potential workmen and supply provisional contracts.

With the advent of so many sites dedicated to making your home look as good as possible, whatever your taste and budget, even the most reluctant decorator is running out of excuses.

www.crownpaint.co.uk
Crown Paints

Overall rating: ★ ★ ★ ★ ★			
Classification:	Company	Readability:	★ ★ ★ ★ ★
Updating:	Monthly	Content:	★ ★ ★ ★
Navigation:	★ ★ ★ ★ ★	Speed:	★ ★ ★ ★

UK

This vibrant, magazine-style website gives a good introduction to Crown's extensive range of paints as well as a wealth of advice on colour trends and decorating ideas. This is no ordinary online experience, but information tempered with funky interactive asides like the colour quiz that tells you what your favourite colour says about your personality. From the lively opening page you can navigate quickly to the site's other areas using the menu bar at the top, or simply browse through the regularly updated features by clicking on the photographs.

SPECIAL FEATURES

Crown Products Choose by Product gives a detailed introduction to the many paints in Crown's extensive range including the Expressions mixing service, metallic paints, woodwash, and Period Colours. For the more adventurous, look out for Decorative Effects, which includes Softsand, a new textured paint, and the Latino collection of modern bright colours with idiosyncratic, colour-non-specific names like Tequila, Sombrero and Iguana. There is also a useful Paint Calculator. Feed in room dimensions, number of doors and windows, and the type of paint you want to use, then select metric or imperial measurements and it will tell you how much paint you will need, helpfully breaking it up into wall and ceiling coverage in case you want to use different colours on each.

Colour Advice Click on the boxes for advice on creating original colour schemes. Project of the Month is themed, for example, into Children's Rooms, Living Rooms, or Kitchens. Stylish room shots are accompanied not only by a list of the paints used, but also by simple advice on pulling together the whole look with textiles and accessories. Top Trends gives good, if a little general, advice on creating modern colour combinations. Using Colour works by clicking on numbers from one to ten for advice from Crown's decorating experts on subjects such as enhancing or compensating for room dimensions and creating a scheme around existing furnishings. These open up in a separate window which makes browsing very easy.

Decorating Advice gives nuts-and-bolts information on the sort of paint suited to particular decorating jobs. Go to Which Paint? and simply roll the cursor over the room diagram to discover what to use on each surface. How To details the top ten decorating questions, from preparing walls to the order in which to paint staircases and windows. Safe Decorating lists lots of practical preparations to make before you even prise open the paint tin.

OTHER FEATURES

News gives details of new ranges, the latest decorating television programmes and pertinent consumer advice. At the time of writing, this included Secrets of Successful House Selling, an imaginative piece which suggested that, in order to make the biggest impact on prospective buyers, you should show them the best room in your house last, not first. You can't order online, but there is a facility to search for your closest store.

Fresh, modern and definitely magnolia-lite, this is a great site. Its speedy navigation isn't compromised by the huge number of gorgeous pictures.

www.homebase.co.uk
Homebase

Overall rating: ★ ★ ★ ★ ★			
Classification:	Company	**Readability:**	★ ★ ★ ★ ★
Updating:	Regularly	**Content:**	★ ★ ★ ★ ★
Navigation:	★ ★ ★ ★ ★	**Speed:**	★ ★ ★ ★

UK 🔒

There's something about shopping in many of the vast DIY warehouses that is forever suffused with the lingering atmosphere of a rainy Sunday afternoon. The explosion of colour on Homebase's exciting site banishes those blues, or mauves, or aquas, forever. Enjoy a fascinating, well-illustrated tour of their enormous range of products and be inspired by the many clever decorating ideas on offer. You can order everything online, including over 1,000 different paint colours, soft furnishings, and hardware. It's very quick and simple to use, so don't log on unless you're prepared to revamp your whole house. It's simply too tempting.

This fresh site is possibly the most sophisticated in its league and is easy to explore. Use the menu bar at the top or the column on the left-hand side of the page to zoom happily from section to section.

SPECIAL FEATURES

Products Use the drop-down menu to choose a department from the 16 on offer. When you enter a section, related links also show up. For example: Curtain Fitments and Blinds brings up relevant Special Offers, Hand Tools, Soft Furnishings, and a Buying Guide to Choosing Curtain Track.

Ideas is divided into Bedrooms, Living Rooms, Children's Rooms, and More Ideas. Each section has several features which outline simple step-by-step instructions to creating a certain look. Handy panels along the right of the screen give links to the products used, from paint and flooring to lighting and ready-made curtains. For the inexperienced DIY-er, there are links to instruction sheets for the skills needed to complete each project.

How-To has admirably clear and straightforward advice for those wishing to tackle decorating or home maintenance projects themselves. Comfortingly, Homebase doesn't presume that you have any previous knowledge and each project is presented in a format you can print out and refer to as you tackle the job. You need Adobe Acrobat to download the files, but if you don't have it, don't worry. Simply click on Get Acrobat to download it. This section also includes Tips and Techniques, which includes a Calculator which opens up on a separate screen to help convert imperial to metric measurements.

OTHER FEATURES

Order Tracking allows customers to trace their orders by typing in an order confirmation number. Products ordered online can be used to collect points on a Homebase Collect and Save card. Special Offers are frequently updated, often seasonal, and spread out evenly between departments.

This beautifully designed and detailed site presents everyday materials with inspirational élan.

www.bbc.co.uk/homes
BBC Online Homes

Overall rating: ★ ★ ★ ★			
Classification:	TV homepage	**Readability:**	★ ★ ★ ★
Updating:	Daily	**Content:**	★ ★ ★
Navigation:	★ ★ ★	**Speed:**	★ ★ ★

UK

If you're addicted to the BBC's many home improvement shows, this web page will provide a virtual fix when they're not on the air. Browse the homepage for regularly updated features or use the menu bar on the left-hand side of the page to see the latest from your favourite programme. As with all BBC sites, this one is clearly designed and packed with content. There is an option to view the site in a text-only format if you have a slow or difficult connection to the Internet, or if you want information rather than pictures. In some cases, it seems as though real, detailed advice has been sacrificed to slick presentation. This site gives you a taster, but doesn't really satisfy anything other than the lightest of decorating appetites.

SPECIAL FEATURES

Changing Rooms Factsheets provides free summaries of techniques used on a programme-to-programme basis. The pictures are very small and so would be of little practical use if you didn't manage to catch the show, but there are clear outlines of techniques and products used. The Projects page provides a little more detailed information and is divided into rooms to speed up the search. Design Bites provides quick tips for instant revamps. Use the pull-down menu at the top of the page for more quick ideas.

DIY SOS is the chirpy, practical site of the television programme presented by Lowri Turner and Nick Knowles.

on the ground here, which is disappointing given the lively nature of the show. The Webguide on the right-hand side has good links if you're still thirsting for information.

OTHER FEATURES

There are also pages on other BBC shows for the conscientious nester. Personal Finance gives advice on mortgages and investing; its Get Talking section goes to enthusiastic advice from empowering, money-managing guru Alvin Hall. Property contains sound advice from the All the Right Moves team on buying, selling, and renting your home. Watchdog covers consumer advice and includes a wonderful Contacts page which contains helpful addresses for the CAB, Office of Fair Trading, and other great sources of advice.

Expert advice is divided into Decorating, Woodwork, Plumbing and so on, with common queries listed under each section. Advice is wide-ranging, from removing stains around the bath to curtain ideas, and although there are no illustrations, the suggestions are clearly written and easy to follow. Step by Step is illustrated, which makes it a little more useful. It has a featured project and a pull-down menu at the top of the page to search through previous projects, such as joining copper pipe or hanging wallpaper. The Tips section is very helpful, with advice on stopping wood from splitting when hammering in a nail to polishing tiles and fitting a skirting board.

Home Front's page is less colourful and expansive than some of the others. Design Outside includes gardening suggestions from the Inside Out team. Disappointingly, it isn't possible to order the Home Front Inside Out booklets online; you have to send a cheque by snail mail to receive them. Feedback takes you to advice on applying to appear on the show; they warn that you need the money and time to take part. Practical and inspirational tips are a little thin

The **Antiques Roadshow** site is reviewed in the Antiques and Architectural Salvage chapter on page 88.

Although this site is a comprehensive and attractive guide to the many BBC home interest shows, it is in some cases vaguely disappointing as depth is sacrificed to breadth.

want to read **more reviews** on this subject?

log on to **www.thegoodwebguide.co.uk**

www.diy.com
B&Q

Overall rating: ★ ★ ★ ★		
Classification: Company	Readability:	★ ★ ★ ★
Updating: Daily	Content:	★ ★ ★ ★ ★
Navigation: ★ ★ ★ ★	Speed:	★ ★ ★ ★

UK

B&Q's cheerful website allows customers to make an online shopping list but, as yet, not to order over the Internet. Use the Search facility on the top-left-hand side of the screen to locate materials quickly. This will bring up a further menu to help you refine your choice by name, make, or price. To browse, use the menu on the left-hand side of the page and if you get lost in the many sections, just click on Home and start again.

SPECIAL FEATURES

Products brings up a menu in dazzling B&Q orange listing their 23 main merchandise areas and outlining a selection of their 40,000 products. If you can't find what you're looking for online, there's a facility to locate your nearest store by postcode or town.

DIY Advice allows customers to ask B&Q's experts for online advice on specific DIY projects. Go to Your Questions Answered to look at detailed step-by-step advice on common home-decorating projects, or use the Ask Our Experts facility to send in your own question. A question we sent in on laying laminate flooring received a response in two working days.

DIY Projects gives clear instructions on how to complete many practical jobs around the house such as Fitting a Door Lock, Wallpapering Techniques, and Basic Plumbing.

OTHER FEATURES

If you're setting aside the weekend to paint your house or put up a shed, check out B&Q's daily weather forecast which scrolls across a box on the top of the homepage. If you have a few moments to browse, go to the bottom of the homepage and click on More Magazine Features to access an archive of articles from Which Online, Livingetc, Ideal Home, Homes & Ideas, Your Garden, and Practical Householder. There's a link to the website of cable channel Discovery Home & Leisure which promises to bring up factsheets and video clips online. Only try out this facility if you have lots of leisure time to spare. There is also a link to Improveline (see p 21).

A vast amount of information and advice clearly displayed, but I haven't seen this much orange since England played Holland at football.

www.dulux.co.uk
Dulux International

Overall rating: ★ ★ ★ ★

Classification:	Company	**Readability:**	★ ★ ★
Updating:	Sporadically	**Content:**	★ ★ ★ ★ ★
Navigation:	★ ★ ★	**Speed:**	★ ★ ★ ★

UK

Dulux's exciting site is simplicity itself to use. As you guide the cursor over the images on the left of the screen, descriptions of what each section contains appear over the Dulux dog's head on the right. Given the vast range of products on offer, this site pulls off the elaborate juggling act of being both informative and inspirational at the same time. Lots of advice, lots of lovely photographs, it goes a long way to convincing you that decorating is fun.

SPECIAL FEATURES

Inspire is Dulux's online lifestyle magazine. Disappointingly, at the time of writing, the features were two months out of date, but there is still plenty to enjoy here. Use the drop-down menu to select archived features, or click on Real Rooms for inspiring shots of customer's homes. These open up in a separate window and are accompanied by plenty of tips on achieving the same look yourself, including step-by-step advice on any paint effects used.

Colour Schemer allows you to select a photograph of a room and then apply different colour schemes to it by clicking on adjacent swatches. Products and colours used in each picture are listed at the bottom of the photograph.

Language of Colour If you're short on inspiration, click on a mood – Warm, Vibrant, Calm, or Fresh – and see a room set decorated in the appropriate style.

Decorating Help Find a Decorator promises to find you a skilled professional whose work is guaranteed by Dulux, and they even – oh joy unbounded – promise that s/he will tidy up. Email your details including when you want the work to start, and they will reply within two working days. When we tried this, we received by return of post the contact numbers of a local decorator who had already been given glowing recommendations by several people. The letter also included helpful suggestions on briefing a decorator and a copy of the Dulux Select Guarantee form which covers work for 12 months.

Discovery encourages you to experiment, and shows the step-by-step process of creating a room scheme, from inspiration to execution, with advice on colour and accessories.

Paint Chooser lets you select by colour or product, and provides helpful alternatives suitable for the finish you require or the surface you're working on.

OTHER FEATURES

You can't purchase paint online, but you can create a Shopping List which you can print out, and then use the Store Finder to find a local stockist. Go to Literature if you would like Dulux to send you free factsheets, colour cards, and special effects postcards. If you just can't wait to get started, you can also download the factsheets.

A visually stimulating and practical site which manages to steer the visitor through the vast range of Dulux products without causing bafflement.

www.englishstamp.com
The English Stamp Company

Overall rating: ★ ★ ★ ★			
Classification: Company		**Readability:**	★ ★ ★ ★
Updating: Frequently		**Content:**	★ ★ ★ ★ ★
Navigation: ★ ★ ★		**Speed:**	★ ★ ★

UK

This site will have you cancelling your plans for the weekend and sitting by the door waiting for the postman. Bright, bold and contemporary, the English Stamp Company produces a range of designs that are hard to resist. You can use their stamps and inks on walls, fabric, and furniture, so they're great for the budget-conscious or time-strapped decorator. Use the I Want To Look At ... facility and scroll down the list to locate products quickly, or use the menu bar on the left-hand side of the page.

The company's ambitions include incorporating real-time video masterclasses and a virtual stamping gallery into their website so that you can experiment with how each design might look in your home, which promises to make a great site even better.

SPECIAL FEATURES

Our Shop View the entire catalogue or limit your search by selecting from the on-screen drop-down menus. The range runs from traditional fleur-de-lis to more contemporary Moorish Squares and abstract Groovy Eggs.

Gallery contains photographs of suitably chic and Elle Deco-looking projects carried out using their stamps. It leaves you marvelling that such cool schemes can be achieved at relatively little cost and with a limited amount of skill.

OTHER FEATURES

Go to Customer Service to view their Frequently Asked Questions and to find out about shipping times and delivery costs. View Our New Products shows their latest stamps and ink colours.

They may be based in a former Dinosaur factory, but there's nothing fossilised about The English Stamp Company's designs. Simple text and lovely photographs make this website one to bookmark.

www.firedearth.com
Fired Earth

Overall rating: ★ ★ ★ ★		
Classification: Company	Readability:	★ ★ ★ ★
Updating: Varies	Content:	★ ★ ★ ★ ★
Navigation: ★ ★ ★	Speed:	★ ★ ★

UK

Fired Earth call themselves the 'interior finishes company',and this website cleverly conveys the luxury, sensuality, and warmth of their paint, rugs, tiles, fabrics, natural flooring, bathroom fittings, and wood. It is only a taster, however. You can order their brochure online for £3.50 to view the full range. A picture menu remains at the top of the page as you browse, making the site simple, if a little slow, to explore. It's one of the few times you don't mind sluggish surfing, there's so many pretty things to look at while you wait.

SPECIAL FEATURES

Inspirations is a wonderful place to introduce yourself to the Fired Earth style. The photographs are themed: A Month in the Country; Elegant; Simplicity, and Wide Open Space. They show how adaptable their materials are to a wide variety of looks, from pared-down contemporary chic to a more classic style.

Products is divided into Paint, Rugs, Natural Flooring, Fabric, Floor Tiles, Wall Tiles and Wood and is deliciously illustrated with wonderfully enticing photography. Click on the images for more details of each range. For example, Paint outlines their five different ranges: the one they produce exclusively with the Victoria & Albert museum, two more from popular decorators Kelly Hoppen and Kevin McCloud, Art Nouveau, and Contemporary. You can order the hand-painted paint card for £5.

Bathrooms is a wonderful demonstration of pure hedonism. Click on the icon to take a virtual tour of one of their new showrooms and zoom in and out to your heart's content on the extensive range of styles.

OTHER FEATURES

News keeps customers up to date with offers and events as well as product launches. Go to Showroom to click on a UK map to find your nearest stockist.

A well-thought-out and beautifully illustrated site. Fired Earth create the kind of products you can imagine living with forever.

www.Homepro.com

HomePro

Overall rating: ★ ★ ★ ★			
Classification:	Service	**Readability:**	★ ★ ★ ★
Updating:	Frequently	**Content:**	★ ★ ★ ★
Navigation:	★ ★ ★ ★	**Speed:**	★ ★ ★

UK

If your idea of a weekend's painting is taking yourself off to the Lake District with some nice heavy paper and a box of watercolours, then perhaps you should get a professional in when it comes to big home decorating projects. You'll find painters, plumbers, builders, electricians, and almost every kind of trades person you can imagine on the HomePro website. Since 1999, they have provided a free service for people looking for a trade professional. They vet everyone on their books extensively, gathering ten referees at random from their files and, when work is completed, getting homeowners to rate the service they've received. In June 2000 they won a Microsoft award for the Best Use of the Internet for Maximising Customer Value.

SPECIAL FEATURES

Find a Pro is the heart of the site. Read their terms and conditions and work guarantee, then register to find a professional. The five-step registration requires you to fill out a few details about the job you need doing and they will come back to you with three contractors in your area prepared to quote for the job. When we tried this, we received the first telephone call from an eager tradesman within two hours, and two more the next day.

Help & Advice provides a good feature on how and why you might want to employ a professional architect or interior designer written by the Evening Standard's David Spittles.

Jargon Buster will allow you to speak to your contractor without feeling like an idiot. It is divided into different trades such as Bricklayer, Electrician, or Roofer, but mysteriously there is no explanation of the exact meaning of a sudden sucking in of air through the teeth.

Forum Click on the house diagram to find questions relevant to your particular problem. You can also register your own question.

OTHER FEATURES

Go to the Shopping page in the Virtual Toolbox to find links to other sites where you can buy tools and equipment. There's also a link to the interiors ezine style revolution.

A clear, useful site which aims to take the headache out of home ownership.

www.improveline.com
Improveline.com

Overall rating: ★ ★ ★ ★			
Classification:	Service	**Readability:**	★ ★ ★ ★
Updating:	Monthly	**Content:**	★ ★ ★ ★ ★
Navigation:	★ ★ ★ ★	**Speed:**	★ ★ ★ ★

UK

Given that there is research stating that DIY projects are one of the major causes of marital upset, there must be lawyers across the land weeping into there claret with the advent of Improveline.com. Their free service finds local, professional workmen and women for all building, decoration and renovation projects. They carry out a four-step screening process on their trades people, examining their credit and legal histories, number of years in business, and customer recommendations. Work is guaranteed for two years with insurers Pinnacle, specialists in building works insurance, to the contract value or £50,000, whichever is the smaller.

It's a very newsy site and its homepage is regularly updated with features on home projects, finance, and the housing market. In July 2000, it was rated as Europe's number one site for home improvement by the Sunday Times E-League.

SPECIAL FEATURES

Project Help Advice contains authoritative advice on making dealings with your contractor go smoothly. Also useful are the Sample Building Repair Contract, Get the Best from your Builder, and How to Tell a Pro from a Con, a great piece on spotting the cowboys.

Financing Your Project allows you to shop for a loan, comparing over 400 different loan providers. In some cases, you can get an instant quote and apply online. We tried to get a quote on a home improvement loan for £5,000 and the search brought up almost 70 lenders, with the APR, monthly repayment and total amount repaid listed in ascending order, making comparison very simple.

OTHER FEATURES

There is a link to the excellent B&Q website (see also p 16) and their Ask the Experts page, as well as numerous links to other suppliers of home-decorating goods.

A well-constructed site that provides a great service to anyone involved in renovating their home

www.paintlibrary.co.uk
Paint & Paper Library

Overall rating: ★ ★ ★ ★		
Classification: Company	**Readability:**	★ ★ ★ ★
Updating: Intermittently	**Content:**	★ ★ ★ ★
Navigation: ★ ★ ★	**Speed:**	★ ★ ★

UK 🔒

This company was founded in 1995 by David Oliver and Sophie Grattan-Bellew and, since then, their exciting and innovative paints and papers have enjoyed well deserved success. They were the first to launch a light-sensitive Metallic, Pearlescent, and Glitter collection, much imitated but never surpassed since. Their range is limited but of the highest quality, and there always seems to be something new to look forward to.

The site is an oasis of calm, cool simplicity in an icon-crazy world. Use the buttons on the left of the page to navigate. You'll feel better for it.

SPECIAL FEATURES

Paint Library Click on the three collections: Original Colours, Architectural, or the Nina Campbell range. To make matching between the collections easier, you can open up a comparison window to see how different paints and papers look next to one another.

Paper Library shows the exotic and unusual Neisha Crossland collection, David Oliver's own Liberation range which includes exciting geometric prints, and Emily Todhunter's mellow, whimsical designs. If the very thought of wallpaper gives you a headache, you'll find the quiet glamour of these quintessentially modern designs very appealing.

Order Charts and Samples Although you can buy paint and paper online, the company strongly advises customers to try them out with sample pots and swatches before making a large order. Sample pieces of wallpaper and printed paint charts are free; sample pots are £2.98 and hand-painted paint charts of their original collection are £8.51. Allow three to five days for delivery.

OTHER FEATURES

David Oliver and his company representatives offer a personal Colour Consultancy service for commercial and residential projects. It is charged at an hourly rate and there is a possibility of discounts on their stock.

If you thought you'd never be the kind of person to buy wallpaper, this site may make you change your mind.

www.stencil-library.com
The Stencil Library

Overall rating: ★ ★ ★ ★			
Classification:	Company	**Readability:**	★ ★ ★ ★
Updating:	Constantly	**Content:**	★ ★ ★ ★ ★
Navigation:	★ ★ ★	**Speed:**	★ ★ ★

UK 🔒

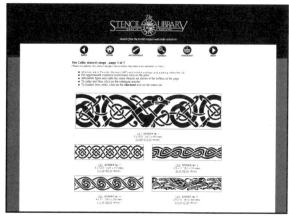

If anyone can save stencilling from itself, it's Helen Morris from The Stencil Library. Over the past few years, this paint effect has had a bad rap. Too many stencils, too poorly designed and too poorly executed: a few crummy cherubs do not a decorative finish make. Helen, however, with her artist's eye and keen sense of the theatrical, continues to innovate, develop and improve.

The site is wonderfully broad in its scope and easy to navigate. Click on the images at the top of the page to move around within the site or simply click on the sun logo to return to the homepage.

SPECIAL FEATURES

Catalogue is divided into 16 sections, including Shaker, Budget, Ottoman, and Garden Room, and covers over 2,000 designs. Stencils are made and cut to order, and many of them can be enlarged or reduced to suit the scale of your room. Ask at the time of ordering.

Hints explains how to produce a professional finish with an extract from Helen Morris' book, The Stencilled Home. It covers cutting stencils, securing them to the wall, dry-brush and oil paint stick stencilling, and shading and blending.

OTHER FEATURES

The Stencil Library also sells an excellent selection of reasonably priced brushes, sponges, spray adhesive, cutting tools, gilding materials, paints, and varnishes in their Accessories section. For the indecisive among you, the site will also save your order for up to five days so you can keep coming back to it with additions or changes before finally submitting it.

Put aside plenty of time to view this site as clicking between the different images is quite addictive. The company's enthusiasm for what they do is catching.

www.casa.co.uk
Casa

Overall rating: ★ ★ ★			
Classification: Company		**Readability:**	★ ★ ★
Updating: Intermittently		**Content:**	★ ★ ★ ★
Navigation: ★ ★ ★		**Speed:**	★ ★ ★

UK 🔒

Once magazine stylists got their hands on Casa's paint in the mid-1990s, they couldn't stop using it and it has spawned many imitators since. Few can rival it, though, for sheer brilliance of colour. The paint is handmade to a traditional Mediterranean recipe using organic pigment and lots of chalk to create their signature rich, matt finish. They still have their 18 key shades and, in league with Paris colour consultants who normally work on fashion trends, they have developed eight new colours. Use the menu bar on the left-hand side of the page to navigate quickly between sections, some of which are rather wordy. Also, more pictures, showing just how lovely Casa's products are, would enhance the site too.

SPECIAL FEATURES

Full Colour Swatch shows yummy tadpole-shaped blotches of Casa's paints. Although Dune, Glacier, and Andalucia look delightful here, they aren't nearly as vibrant as they look in real life.

Mix Your Own Colours Casa's playful, innovative philosophy is well served by their latest wheeze: mixing your own paint. In the majority of Homebase stores, you'll find handpainted samples of their 18 colours, plus samples of eight new colours created by mixing quantities of the established range. They urge customers to mix Casa Blanca (white) with their vibrant colours to create delicious, intense pastels.

Paint Effects demonstrates the adaptability of Casa's range. With the right preparation and finishing, you can use it on walls, furniture, tiles, and even on radiators. The paint comes in concentrated form and you can use it neat for intense colour or diluted with water to achieve different effects. They give advice on the suggested levels of dilution for rolling, sponging or dry brushing. The 125ml Minipots are big enough to tackle a small piece of furniture.

OTHER FEATURES

Go to Order Online and scroll down the page to see the order form. There's a minimum order of £14.99, but postage and packing are free. You can also order a free, printed catalogue by email or send three first class stamps for 26 hand-painted colour chips. The Stockists list is heavily weighted towards the south of England, but there is a link to Homebase who also carry their paints.

Casa's range of ravishing paint colours are not shown at their best on this rather text-heavy site. A little editing and a few more pictures could redress the balance nicely.

www.painted-house.com

Debbie Travis' Painted House

Overall rating: ★ ★ ★			
Classification: TV homepage		**Readability:**	★ ★ ★
Updating: Intermittently		**Content:**	★ ★ ★
Navigation: ★ ★ ★ ★		**Speed:**	★ ★ ★ ★

US

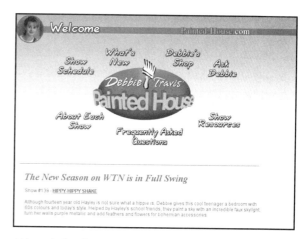

The New Season on WTN is in Full Swing

Show #139 · HIPPY HIPPY SHAKE

Although fourteen year old Hayley is not sure what a hippie is, Debbie gives this cool teenager a bedroom with 60s colours and today's style. Helped by Hayley's school friends, they paint a sky with an incredible faux skylight, turn her walls purple metallic and add feathers and flowers for bohemian accessories.

Based around decorator Debbie Travis' US television show, this site is a good source of practical tips for transforming your home. She covers everything, from basic instructions on painting over tiles to more decorative projects such as making your own chandelier. Once you get past all of the television show hoopla and invitations to buy Debbie's videotapes, the advice is sound and clearly expressed.

SPECIAL FEATURES

About Each Show The shows are listed in numerical order with a simple description. Click on a subject that piques your interest and an instruction sheet will appear in a new browser window. To return to the list, simply close the new window. The shows are themed. For example, Working from Home, gives a nifty facelift to an old filing cabinet, Suburban Kitchen demonstrates a country-style makeover, and Santa Fe Family Room shows a room transformed by simple techniques such as stencilling, bleaching wood, and creating a decoupage coffee table.

FAQ Click on List of Questions to go to a menu of popular queries, such as: can I paint my melamine cabinets? or can you share some tips on caring for brushes? The advice is clear and easy to follow, and any good DIY or hardware store would be able to advise on alternative products where the ones used by Debbie Travis are exclusively American.

Although the site may not be the most visually arresting on the internet, there are lots of effective, cheap tips on transforming rooms and furniture with techniques which you don't have to be a creative dynamo to use.

www.dupontsmartpaint.com
Du Pont SmartPaint

Overall rating: ★ ★ ★			
Classification: Company		**Readability:**	★ ★ ★ ★
Updating: Frequently		**Content:**	★ ★ ★ ★ ★
Navigation: ★ ★ ★		**Speed:**	★ ★ ★

UK

If planning your decorating scheme is driving you wild with frustration, this site may help you inject some fun into the process. Bringing a little interaction to the interior, Du Pont's site allows you to experiment with room schemes and gives succinct advice on everything from surface preparation to colour selection. Much is made of their new brand, SmartPaint, which is marketed through B&Q and can be used on almost any surface, including walls, woodwork, and metal. Cheerful, bright and playful, the site can at first seem overwhelmingly busy, but it's simple to return to the homepage and start again if you get a little lost. Otherwise, use the panel at the top to navigate between each section, or if you have a specific query, use the Ask SmartPaint box at the top of the screen.

SPECIAL FEATURES

Colour Lab Select a room you would like to paint by clicking on the house diagram or selecting from the drop-down menu. Next, you can play with colour schemes by clicking between their chosen combinations or creating your own using the Custom Colours Selection. This part of the site is quite speedy as the graphic is rather crude and, though it is quite good fun, transferring ideas you come up with here to a real room scheme would be rather difficult.

Design Inspiration contains practical advice for all decorators, from short-term renters to homeowners with rather more money to spend.

Oops runs through a list of common decorating problems, from preparation to cleaning up.

Smart Painting ABCs The basics, including Top 10 Questions, Tool Types and Applying Paints.

Working with a Decorator is a very useful section for those considering employing a professional decorator for the first time. It contains a Checklist of relevant questions, such as level of experience, qualifications and how they would approach your job, with three columns for each of the quotations you should seek before employing anyone. For Your Contract runs through the kind of legal guidelines you should follow with your designer.

A very busy site crammed with sound advice. The aesthetic is more functional than inspirational and it is difficult to see how the colour-scheming plans could be transferred to a real room.

www.farrow-ball.co.uk

Farrow & Ball

Overall rating: ★ ★ ★

Classification:	Company	Readability:	★ ★ ★ ★
Updating:	Regularly	Content:	★ ★ ★
Navigation:	★ ★ ★ ★	Speed:	★ ★ ★

UK

Farrow & Ball was making historically correct colours when other companies still thought oatmeal and apple white were the last word in wall-wear. They developed their colours initially for the National Trust and then brought the range to a wider public in smart, suitably old-fashioned looking tins. Some of paints are named after the stately homes for which they were developed, but others have intriguing and irresistible names such as Mouse's Back, Pigeon, Dead Salmon and String. If the recent trend for vibrant, Mediterranean colours makes your head hurt, rest your eyes on these calm and beautiful shades which are perfectly suited to the UK's cold Northern light.

SPECIAL FEATURES

Product Information gives information on their elegant range of papers, paints, and glazes with a brief description of their application and coverage. Check on the listing in the Finish column for more extensive details. It would be very helpful if prices were listed here too, and not just in the online Shopping section.

Requesting Samples gives two choices: free, printed colour cards and A4 wallpaper samples or, for about £6, painted colour cards, sample colour books and sample pots of paint from their own range and that of Jane Churchill. Go to the Read the Farrow & Ball Colour Selection Guide before using the Click Here ordering link. Pictures of the samples could be

bigger but, as they wisely suggest, it would be inadvisable to order a huge batch of paint before trying it out with a sample pot anyway.

OTHER INFORMATION

To find your nearest Stockists, use the scroll bar to select your county. Not all counties are represented, so if you're having trouble finding a supplier click on the Order Online or Contact Us link to assuage your thirst for historic colours. What's New at Farrow & Ball gives information of new products and stockists.

Farrow & Ball is a wonderful company with an exciting range of materials for decorators with a classic leaning. Their site could do with a gentle overhaul to allow it to do more justice to the uniqueness of their products.

OTHER SITES OF INTEREST

Don't forget sites in the Soft Furnishings and Finishing Touches chapter such as:

Designers Guild
www.designersguild.com

Jane Churchill
www.athome.co.uk

Sanderson
www.sanderson-uk.com

Scumble Goosie
www.scumble-goosie.co.uk

Or from the Learning chapter:

Annie Sloan School of Decoration
www.anniesloan.com

Criterion Tiles and The Reject Tile Shop
www.criterion-tiles.co.uk
Criterion Tiles is a London-based company which sells a wide variety of unusual tiles, sourced from big manufacturers right down to individual potters. The traditional sits easily along side the innovative: hand-painted, encaustic, and relief-moulded tiles, mosaic, marble, glass and metal, there's a wealth of choice you won't find in many other places. Their sister company, The Reject Tile Shop, carries second-quality, discontinued, and special purchase tiles at bargain prices. There is no brochure as their stock changes constantly, but in person or over the telephone, they offer a great deal of experience and helpful, patient advice.

Decorating Your Home
www.decorating-your-home.com
This American site offers sensible, inexpensive decorating tips following their 'Use what you have' philosophy. The art

of arranging your furniture or making the most of unused space in your kitchen takes precedence over extensive shopping lists or major renovation projects. The column on the left-hand side of the screen allows you to choose the room you want to focus on and then takes you to brief, illustrated features. Videoclips load into a separate window, but they are quite slow and don't really give you anything more than you can get by simply viewing the pages. Table lamps and candles are key to their styling philosophy, but there are plenty of other ideas too.

Decorator Secrets
www.decoratorsecrets.com
A very approachable and easy-to-follow site which is short on illustrations but strong on practical advice for the budget decorator. Quick Tips, Top Ten Do's and Don'ts, and the How Do I? sections are good for the flummoxed beginner. Also worth a look is the Just Ask It! Forum, particularly the General Decorating Forum. You can also register to receive their free What's Hot newsletter each month.

Design-Online
www.design-online.co.uk
This site is home to The Interior Design Information Service which primarily provides a sourcing facility for the interior decorating trade. Click on the globe logo to enter the site. Given the subject matter, the layout and design are a little basic but it could be a useful first stop if you are looking for a local interior designer. Their list provides contact details, and a brief description of the kind of work the designers generally undertake, as well as links to their websites if they have one.

DIYFixit
www.diyfixit.co.uk
Want to hang a door? Replace the cord in a sash window? Deal with a frozen pipe? DIYFixit offers clearly written, simply illustrated advice on a wide range of home improvement projects. Use the icons along the top of the page to go to

rooms, such as bathroom or kitchen, and a selection of common projects you might undertake there, or use the column on the left-hand side of the page to explore specific skills such as plumbing or electrics.

DoItYourself.com

www.doityourself.com

A huge US website dedicated to home improvement. Use the menu across the top of the page to browse through general categories such as Repair/Fix-It, Decorate and Outdoors, or use the keyword search. Advice is well presented and easy to follow. There is a large Community Forum section if you would like to post your own query, and the Editor's Choice Web Links are extensive too.

Just Doors

www.justdoors.co.uk

If your kitchen is looking tired but you can't face the chaos, or don't have the cash, to remodel it completely, simply changing the doors could be a solution. Just Doors' simple website provides an introduction to their service. Their inexpensive, custom-made doors come in three different styles – Fielded Panel, Tongue and Groove, and Shaker Style – making them best suited to a classic or country look. They take all the boring work out of it too. The MDF doors arrive primed and sanded, leaving you to do the fun part of painting them in your chosen colour. Delivery usually takes a couple of weeks and is free for orders over £100.

Screwfix Direct

www.screwfix.com

Screwfix Direct began life as a supplier to the building trade, but these days whether you want to buy 200 paintbrushes or just two, they provide a great online ordering service for builders and homeowners alike. The no-nonsense site offers customers a full online catalogue on the same day as they publish the paper version – no 'edited highlights' here. If you are looking for a particular item, use the fast and accurate search engine. If you prefer to order a catalogue you can, and still use the online facility as a fast, convenient way of compiling and sending your order. The Express Checkout facility is incredibly simple to use, and helpfully provides a running total of the value of your order and highlights discounts. If you place your order before five o'clock in the afternoon, the goods will usually be with you the next working day. Although it is primarily a great way to take the frustration out of shopping for the more mundane tools and materials you may need to complete a home renovation project, the Refurbishment section also includes some more decorative items such as curtain poles, cabinet doors, flooring, fires, coving, and timber decking.

soft furnishings & finishing touches

Generating original room schemes has never been easier. There are products and materials available on almost every high street now, and certainly on the cyber high street, that ten years ago were available only to professional decorators or from obscure specialist shops. Customer demand, lead by glossy magazines and television how-to programmes, has generated huge improvements in the range and variety of furnishing materials now available to the average shopper.

Of course, browsing on the web does not allow you to rub a swatch of fabric against your face to feel its texture or to sink into a sofa, but it can help busy decorators to both widen and narrow their searches at the same time. It expands the sheer number of ranges you can view in making your choice, and limits the amount of time you need to spend on fruitless shopping trips looking at entirely unsuitable materials.

On the level playing field of the internet, it is interesting to note that, in many cases, small companies outstrip their bigger brothers and sisters in retailing in the sheer imagination and scope of their sites. They have seized the opportunity that the web offers to display their products and services innovatively, and frequently put much bigger marketing operations to shame.

Some of the larger companies' websites seem almost like an afterthought. There's a lot of 'oh, we have to have one of those,' but not much ingenuity or thoughtfulness in the presentation. This will only change as customers become more web-savvy and start to expect useful company sites as a further element of good customer service. As in all things, if you demand more you usually get more.

www.thewhiteco.com
The White Company

Overall rating: ★ ★ ★ ★ ★			
Classification:	Ecommerce	Readability:	★ ★ ★ ★
Updating:	Constantly	Content:	★ ★ ★ ★ ★
Navigation:	★ ★ ★ ★ ★	Speed:	★ ★ ★

UK 🔒

You can find absolutely everything you might ever want in The White Company's wonderful range of home furnishings and accessories, so long as it's white. If that thought makes you nervous, don't worry; this catalogue will banish any thoughts you ever had that white was bland. Wonderful finishes, textures, and detailing make their products exciting and eminently covetable. The site is easy to navigate, with a menu on the left-hand side and icons for ordering, with more information and other queries at the bottom of every page. They have an exemplary commitment to customer service, with products being dispatched within 24 hours when they are in stock. This is online shopping at its best.

SPECIAL FEATURES

Bedrooms contains everything you need for a good night's sleep. Browse through Bedlinen, Bedspreads, Throws, Duvets, and Pillows. The Linen Cupboard is useful for some hard-to-find items such as iron-on size tags to make identifying bedding easier, mattress protectors, and anti-allergy bedding.

Bathrooms includes sumptuous bath towels, of course, and other chic accessories such as divine cashmere hot-water bottle covers and socks, laundry bags, and cotton waffle slippers.

Dining Rooms Look no further for all of the ingredients for the well-dressed table: linen, china, glassware, and accessories, including napkin rings and storm lanterns. There is even a book on folding napkins to make every dinner at home a celebration.

Gifts and Accessories includes For Him, For Her, For Weddings, and For Children and Babies. Start your Christmas shopping here, and you may never have to look elsewhere.

Furniture The White Company had so many enquiries from customers about the pieces they used to prop their photography, they decided to bring out their own range of furniture. Choose from their refined collection of bedside tables, bedheads, children's furniture, and lamps.

OTHER FEATURES

The White Company's enthusiasm for what they do shines through on every page. Special Offers outlines frequently-updated bargains of up to 50 per cent off, available to web customers only. Special Services includes gift vouchers, gift wrapping, and wedding lists guests can access straight off the net. Sign In allows customers to create their own profile to make shopping easier, or simply to register to receive a monthly email about special offers. You can also request a catalogue, but why would you want to? The White Company makes online shopping a pleasure.

An exemplary website which manages to pull off the all-too-rare achievement of outstripping their paper catalogue in terms of style, simplicity and ease of ordering.

www.designersguild.com
Designers Guild

Overall rating: ★ ★ ★ ★			
Classification:	Company	**Readability:**	★ ★ ★
Updating:	Seasonally	**Content:**	★ ★ ★ ★
Navigation:	★ ★ ★ ★	**Speed:**	★ ★ ★

UK

The homepage tells us 'it's a way of life' and, after a few moments browsing this site, you'll really wish it was. Beautiful photography of exquisitely styled rooms confirms that Tricia Guild continues to do what she does best; constantly updating her lines to keep them at the forefront of modern design while maintaining her signature style. Indeed, there are many photographs of the tousled-haired one, barefoot and lolling artfully on one of the many chic yet comfortable sofas.

The website focuses on new lines rather than the older ranges. Use the menu on the left to enter the part of the site which interests you. Once you start to browse, the menu remains along the bottom of the page making switching between sections very simple. Once inside a section, there are no thumbnails, so you have to subject yourself to the entire DG experience to locate something that may appeal to you.

SPECIAL FEATURES

Products is divided into six sections covering the Guild empire. Fabric & Wallpaper is the largest section. Use the Next button on the lower right-hand side of the page to move from one luscious picture to another. It's a dazzling banquet of deep reds, ochres, aubergines, greens, and blues; the one feature that links them is the intensity and clarity of colour. Even the pastel shades are vibrant and demonstrate admirably that paler colours can have dramatic decorative impact. Refreshingly, fabrics are shown on modern as well as antique furniture, showing how suitable these ranges are for both. Furniture introduces a limited but smart range of pieces, which confirms that comfort and elegance are not mutually exclusive. Bed & Bath is a tour through Designers Guild's extensive selection of bedlinen, where the ubiquitous white is joined by more bold and colourful designs. Accessories runs the whole gamut, from cushions and throws to stationery and bags as curvy and enticing as a DG sofa. Designers Guild Kids lightens the mix of exquisite, grown-up luxury with a little whimsy. Emily Todhunter's range of fabrics and wallpapers is manufactured and distributed by Designers Guild. They are admirable for their calm, elegant restraint, giving them a timeless quality.

OTHER FEATURES

Click on Stockists to find your nearest retailer; not every county is represented, but there is a good spread across the country. If you are searching for a particular fabric, Swatches takes you to a page of artfully displayed shopping bags with the names of fabrics and wallpapers above them. Click to show small swatches. UK Mail Order looks very tempting, but is merely an invitation to send in £3 for a catalogue, which is refundable against your first purchase.

No prices, no mail order, but it's probably just as well. Tricia Guild's products are impossible to resist.

www.damask.co.uk
Damask

Overall rating: ★ ★ ★ ★			
Classification:	Company	Readability:	★ ★ ★ ★
Updating:	Twice a year	Content:	★ ★ ★ ★ ★
Navigation:	★ ★ ★ ★	Speed:	★ ★ ★

UK

Damask creates all of the necessary ingredients for totally delicious bedrooms, right down to nightdresses and room scents. They describe their range as 'contemporary classics for the home', and manage to pull off the difficult feat of creating quintessentially pretty designs without the merest risk of entering into the realms of the twee. Their country house classics would breathe a little fresh air into the grandest town house or most rustic cottage.

Use the menu down the left-hand side of the page to navigate between sections and to see a summary of what each part contains. Click on the delightful images to enlarge them and get more details.

SPECIAL FEATURES

Home Collection opens up several choices. Irresistibly romantic Bedspreads come with jacquard patterns, scallop-edges, and lace edging, in white, cream, and a selection of beautiful pastels. Bedlinen is luxurious with smart details such as blue or pink edging, hemstitched borders, and satin finish in some cases. The quilts are reminiscent of the ones you wish your granny had left you. Pretty florals, toiles de jouy, retro patterns, and rich, dramatic colours sit comfortably side by side. Fine towels come in soft colours with Damask's signature jacquard borders, and can be bought in gift or wedding sets.

Decorative Accessories and Gifts demonstrate Damask's clever combination of the traditional and modern. The Byron writing desk would be equally useful for penning billets-doux or for holding your laptop while you work. The breakfast trays, side tables, cushion covers, and throws provide stylish finishing touches.

OTHER FEATURES

Nursery and Children's contains charming pint-sized quilts and nightclothes, suitable for ages six months to ten years. Ladies' Sleepwear and Loungewear are wonderfully crisp, cool, and easy to wear. There is also a new collection of Home Fragrances, in Damask Rose, Lavender and Neroli. If they smell as good as the rest looks, they are destined for enormous success. Go to Contact Us to find out about the telephone and postal mail order service.

A well-designed and beautifully illustrated site which is almost as enjoyable as browsing through Damask's London shop. Online ordering would make it even more attractive.

www.thedormyhouse.com
The Dormy House

Overall rating: ★ ★ ★ ★			
Classification:	Company	Readability:	★ ★ ★ ★
Updating:	Intermittently	Content:	★ ★ ★ ★
Navigation:	★ ★ ★ ★	Speed:	★ ★ ★

UK

The Dormy House has come a long way since this family firm started selling round chipboard tables in 1983. Now they manufacture a fantastic range of co-ordinated furniture which you can either paint or upholster yourself, or have them do it for you. The site provides a comprehensive, easily navigable introduction to their stock. Unfortunately, you can't order online yet, but given their strong commitment to customer service, it surely can't be long in coming.

SPECIAL FEATURES

About the Dormy House details their many products and services. Buy their pieces uncovered to work on yourself, or use their comprehensive finishing service. Customers are invited to send in their own fabrics or allow The Dormy House to source one for them. They will send you swatches to choose from or, if you already have a pattern in mind, they can order it for you direct from the designer.

Product Range It would be difficult not to find something you might find useful in their extensive range of products. Click on the words beneath the strip of photographs or click on the menu on the left-hand side of the page to bring up a detailed list of choices. Some highlights are their ottomans which are adapted to hold A4 files inside, negating the need for an ugly filing cabinet in your home-office, and the wide selection of screens, from large room dividers to simple MDF fire screens. Softer furnishings, such as padded headboards and quilted bedspreads, made from your own fabric or one sourced by them are also very popular.

OTHER FEATURES

Order a Catalogue allows customers to email for a detailed colour brochure. If you find something you like, fill in the Order Enquiry Form, and a member of staff will telephone to discuss finish and payment. Orders are dispatched between seven to 28 days. They also provide a Painting Service, if you have a particular design in mind but are nervous about putting brush to MDF.

A useful and enjoyable site, and a must for the home decorator keen to source customised finishing touches.

www.housenet.com
HouseNet

Overall rating: ★ ★ ★ ★			
Classification:	Ezine	**Readability:**	★ ★ ★ ★
Updating:	Continuously	**Content:**	★ ★ ★ ★
Navigation:	★ ★ ★ ★	**Speed:**	★ ★ ★

US

HouseNet's site is bright and straightforward, full of tips, how-tos, step-by-steps, and free advice on almost everything to do with the home and garden. For our purposes, it provides quick and inexpensive soft furnishing ideas using readily-available materials.

SPECIAL FEATURES

Sewing Ideas View a weekly craft project for the home. If this week's confection does not appeal to you, use the drop-down menu of Great Projects to Make. Home Furnishings contains lots of simple ideas for making your own valances, pillowcases, lampshades, shower curtains, and table runners. Each one has an indication of the level of skill required, although the instructions are so clear and well illustrated you could probably make a fairly good attempt at them even if you've never sewn on anything more complicated than a button. Discover some good tips for a professional finish by clicking on the cotton reel logos.

Message Boards are of a higher standard than most, as they are monitored by a home-furnishing professional. Grouped into eight sections, use them to ask for advice, or exchange ideas with other busy-fingered web users.

A well-constructed site with lots of sound home-sewing advice and inspiration.

www.jim-lawrence.co.uk
Jim Lawrence Traditional Ironwork

Overall rating: ★ ★ ★ ★			
Classification: Company		Readability:	★ ★ ★ ★
Updating: Regularly		Content:	★ ★ ★ ★ ★
Navigation: ★ ★ ★ ★ ★		Speed:	★ ★ ★

UK

www.Christopher-Wray.com
Christopher Wray Lighting

Overall rating: ★ ★ ★			
Classification: Company		Readability:	★ ★ ★
Updating: Intermittently		Content:	★ ★ ★
Navigation: ★ ★ ★		Speed:	★ ★ ★ ★

UK

The site of this family-run Suffolk ironmongers manages to combine modern technology with an ancient craft as though it were the most natural thing in the world. Their handmade, traditional products are admirably displayed and easily located. Customers can download free upgrades for Microsoft Internet Explorer and Netscape Navigator by clicking on How To Get The Most Out Of This Site on the homepage. Explore the site by clicking on Take A Look At Our Online Catalogue and selecting from the ranges listed at the bottom of the page, or go to Find Out More About Jim Lawrence for an overview of the styles and finishes in their product range.

SPECIAL FEATURES

Finishes describes the admirable variety of choices they provide for customers. Select between: polished gun metal or pewter style; old ivory painted finish; matt old gold; brass; matt black; verdigris, and traditional beeswax.

Showroom guides customers through their range of curtain poles, door handles, kitchen and bathroom fittings, wall lights, lamps, and outdoor lanterns. Click on the letter icon to read customer testimonials in a pop-up window.

A lively and well-constructed site which balances arresting illustrations and succinct, easily accessible information.

Christopher Wray is one of the UK's biggest decorative lighting suppliers and this site provides a good introduction to the company's 6,000 products and accessories. Clicking on the main area of the homepage takes you to the catalogue order form, so use the menu on the left-hand side of the page to get an idea of the range of stock on offer.

SPECIAL FEATURES

Highlights gives a selection of lighting in different categories, including bathroom lighting, floor lamps, picture lights, and wall lights. Whether you're looking for sleek modern lights or something to go with a more classical scheme, the chances are you can find something here to suit you. Click on the thumbnails to discover more details about each piece.

Antique Lighting Christopher Wray began his career selling reconditioned antique lamps before becoming a more general lighting retailer, so he has a particular sensitivity for older lighting. This is perhaps the country's best source for old-style fittings such as switches and flex, which comes in eight different colours. The company also provides a Repair & Restoration Service for old and new lighting and, having used this service several times, we can vouch for the efficiency and thoughtfulness of their staff. They also convert suitable objects such as vases and jars into lamps.

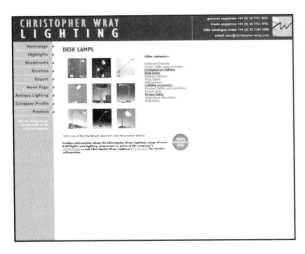

www.thecurtainexchange.cwc.net
The Curtain Exchange

Overall rating: ★ ★ ★			
Classification:	Company	**Readability:**	★ ★ ★
Updating:	Varies	**Content:**	★ ★ ★
Navigation:	★ ★ ★	**Speed:**	★ ★ ★

UK

What began as the inspired idea of friends who wanted to find a way of making some money while raising their young families is now a great success, with a dozen stores and franchises from Boston Spa in West Yorkshire to Launceston in Cornwall. You can't buy online, but the site provides a comprehensive guide to their services.

OTHER FEATURES

The Order Catalogue service provides a secure online ordering system. The hefty 244-page colour catalogue costs £7.95 including postage and packing, and includes a £5 voucher redeemable on the first purchase. Customers can also email for a free exterior lighting brochure and use the Stockists button to find out the nearest of Christopher Wray's 18 showrooms.

A helpful and clearly illustrated introduction to Christopher Wray's vast range of decorative lighting.

SPECIAL FEATURES

Buying Secondhand If you're worried about buying someone else's curtains, don't be. They're all carefully checked and cleaned, and many come from show houses, interior designers' displays, or are cancelled orders, so in some cases they have never even experienced the daily wear and tear of a real home. Expect designer fabrics and a high degree of finish, with linings and/or interlining as standard. The curtains are displayed around the walls of the shops with their measurements clearly displayed on the labels. You can take curtains home on approval to make sure they will go with your scheme, and alterations can be done in house.

Selling Secondhand Curtain Exchange will sell on everything, from very grand drawing room extravaganzas, complete with swags, tails and tie-backs, to simple pairs of small, well-made cotton curtains. If your drapes are acceptable and you agree on a price, they will display them in one of their shops for six months. If they find a buyer, expect a cheque for about half of the selling price. Curtain Exchange can also collect your curtains, do on-site evaluations and arrange dry cleaning for a small fee.

OTHER FEATURES

Curtain Exchange also sells Readymade Curtains from its own range of over 40 designs, with new designs being added twice a year. The Bespoke Curtains service allows customers to choose from their wide range of designer fabrics and create a special scheme around their existing furnishings. There are many accessories available, from tie-backs and padded bulletin boards, to footstools and cushions, to help to complete the finished look. Branches helps you to find your nearest shop by clicking on a map of the UK.

A good introduction to the Curtain Exchange's service, although a few more photographs would lift the site enormously.

www.habitat.co.uk
Habitat

Overall rating: ★ ★ ★			
Classification:	Company	**Readability:**	★ ★ ★
Updating:	Regularly	**Content:**	★ ★
Navigation:	★ ★ ★	**Speed:**	★ ★

UK

This site contains too few pictures and too little information to justify its slowness. But it is pretty, in a self-consciously modern way, and provides a glimpse of Habitat's latest ranges. You can choose to view with Shockwave or without. Click on the Habitat logo on the top right of the homepage or, more simply, use the drop-down Direct Access menu to continue your search. Alternatively, once inside the site, use the list of departments along the bottom of the page.

SPECIAL FEATURES

Lounging Click on Sofas, Armchairs, Side Tables, Beds, or Storage to view a limited range of well-designed modern furniture in each category. In Sofas, for example, a large image appears with a range of fabric swatches on the right-hand side. Click on the colour that appeals to you to enlarge and get a better idea of shade and texture. Other designs appear in duotone photographs along the bottom of the page. Run the cursor along them to see a full-colour photograph and click on them for more details.

Everyday Things includes a limited selection of accessories in Vases, Lights and Rugs.

OTHER FEATURES

Customers can register on News Letter to receive free monthly updates on trends, features, and special issues.

Like the rest of this site, Free Catalogue promises much but delivers little. Apparently, the catalogue is 'flooded with ideas'; a pity more of them didn't trickle down onto this site. Maddeningly, you have to fill out a form, print it off, and present it at your local store to receive a free catalogue, with that irritating proviso, 'while stocks last'. Don't Habitat realise that, with a more efficient website, they wouldn't have to go to the trouble and expense of publishing quite so many tree-hungry catalogues? Find a Store is helpful, however, as it includes opening times, the name of the store manager, and local landmarks to help you locate it.

A rather self-conscious site which offers little more than a few pretty pictures. It provides a snapshot of the latest ranges but would need considerable expansion to make it really useful.

www.marks-and-spencer.co.uk
Marks & Spencer

Overall rating: ★ ★ ★			
Classification:	Company	Readability:	★ ★ ★
Updating:	Varies	Content:	★ ★ ★ ★
Navigation:	★ ★ ★	Speed:	★ ★ ★ ★

UK

Although Marks & Spencer's website is relatively easy to navigate, it is vaguely underwhelming in its presentation. It has the clean, fresh layout so popular with purveyors of modern design, but none of the inspirational room shots to add a little life to the site. Dozens and dozens of pleasing-enough pictures give a good introduction to Marks & Spencer's stock, but do not endow its products with the sort of must-have appeal of some of the more stylish sites.

Click on Home at the top of the homepage to look at furnishings. Although pictures are small, click on them to bring up an enlargement in a pop-up window. Ordering is straightforward and a running total appears on the top right-hand side of the screen so you can keep an eye on your spending. Order up until seven in the evening, and they aim to deliver the goods to you within 48 hours. Delivery charges are a reasonable £2.95 per order.

SPECIAL FEATURES

Home is the place to start shopping for furniture and furnishings. Bedrooms comprises 11 pages of bedlinen with co-ordinating curtains, lampshades, smart seagrass laundry baskets, duvets, pillows, and quilted bedcovers. The smallness of the pictures does make the pages appear a little like an explosion in a pastel factory, but there are plenty of chenilles, waffle weaves, and chambray to give the collection a broader appeal.

Ready-made curtains are one of the great retailing successes of the past decade, and Marks & Spencer have done more than most to perpetuate the no-sew trend. In their Curtain section choose from five pages of plain tab-headed panels, more traditional florals, sheers, damasks, and linens, along with accessories such as curtain poles and the ubiquitous curtain clips.

OTHER FEATURES

The selection of Furniture is limited online. You might have to satisfy your urge for change by selecting from the collection of Throws & Cushions, which includes embroidered wool, velvets, and animal prints. Bathroom contains a selection of high-quality towels in a number of shades and other accessories such as bath mats and shower curtains. The Rugs section is particularly good for subdued, modern designs.

A wide range of stock rather unimaginatively displayed. A few more atmospheric or inspirational photographs would make this a much more appealing site.

www.osborneandlittle.com
Osborne & Little

Overall rating: ★ ★ ★			
Classification:	Company	Readability:	★ ★ ★ ★
Updating:	Seasonally	Content:	★ ★ ★
Navigation:	★ ★ ★ ★	Speed:	★ ★ ★ ★

UK

Log on to this elegant site for news of the latest ranges from this smart interiors company. On entering the site, customers are invited to view a Macromedia Flash presentation of the world according to Osborne & Little. If you have five minutes to spare, click continue, if not, hit skip to go to their menu page.

Begun in 1968 by brothers-in-law Peter Osborne and Antony Little, the firm continues to reinterpret modern trends in their own distinctively chic manner. They now market ranges by Nina Campbell and Liberty, which are included in their site.

SPECIAL FEATURES

Osborne & Little's page is divided into prints, weaves, and wallpapers. Click on the photographs to find out more about a range which interests you. As with the other pages, information comes up in a separate pop-up window and allows you to view other papers or fabrics in your chosen range in all of their colourways.

Nina Campbell consistently reinvents her comfortable, country house style with considerable panache. Styles range from pretty to bold; her range of opulent gold and silver wallpapers is particularly distinctive.

Liberty designs retain their characteristic Arts & Crafts style with a range of botanically-inspired papers and fabrics in rich, earthy colours.

OTHER FEATURES

Click on the Stockists button and then select your chosen county to find the retailer closest to you.

The site provides a good snapshot of current trends reinterpreted for the smart end of the decorating market.

www.rogeroates.com
Roger Oates Design

Overall rating: ★ ★ ★			
Classification:	Company	**Readability:**	★ ★ ★
Updating:	Regularly	**Content:**	★ ★ ★ ★
Navigation:	★ ★ ★	**Speed:**	★ ★ ★

UK

Roger Oates makes exquisite modern carpets and runners in linen, wool, and sisal. Some of his pieces are part of the permanent collections of the Victoria & Albert Museum and the Crafts Council. You can obtain your own design classic from their shops in London and Herefordshire, or browse through their elegantly shot online catalogue.

The site is beautifully illustrated, but navigation is a little slow and cumbersome, with lots of clicking the back button to get to a selection menu. From the homepage, click on the pictures to move into a particular section and then use the drop-down menus to refine your search. In some cases, click on the white circle which appears in the main pictures and a pop-up screen will appear with a close- up of the carpet in question.

SPECIAL FEATURES

Rugs & Runners are the heart of Roger Oates' Collection. Whatever your scheme or style, you are bound to find something among these beautifully made and designed pieces to complement it. They are remarkably versatile, as is Mr Oates' team. Some of the runners can be sewn together to make larger rugs and all are sold by the linear metre, with bound or fringed edges to match your requirements. Particularly interesting is the Antiqued Cotton collection, full of cheerful stripes with a whiff of the seaside about them contemporary wool and jute blends, and delicious award winning confections in wool felt. The smart Venetian range of runners is reversible and dry-cleanable, making them great value.

OTHER FEATURES

Contact gives phone numbers to call for mail order details. Customers don't appear to be able to order online yet, but from experience we can vouch for Roger Oates Design's high level of customer service, including sending out swatches of carpets you may be interested in. Studio Shop offers an almost irresistible invitation to visit their shop in Herefordshire. As well as the signature rugs and runners, the shop carries ranges of glassware, tableware, bed and bathroom furnishings, garden accessories, and a special children's range.

A rather slow site with no online ordering as yet, but worth persevering with because of the loveliness of the products on offer.

www.sanderson-uk.com
Sanderson

Overall rating: ★ ★ ★			
Classification:	Company	**Readability:**	★ ★ ★ ★
Updating:	Seasonally	**Content:**	★ ★ ★
Navigation:	★ ★ ★ ★	**Speed:**	★ ★ ★

UK

Sanderson have made large strides in the past few years to give their collections a broader appeal. Of course, you can still use their products to recreate a sort of Merchant Ivory view of the past, but there are plenty of relaxed stripes and checks and stylized florals suitable for a more modern, more informal style of decorating.

The site provides a taster of their latest collections, but without prices, which might have made it a little more useful. Pictures can be enlarged in a pop-up window which, at the time of writing, did not prove to be wholly reliable. The menu remains along the bottom of the screen whatever page you're on, making navigation easy.

SPECIAL FEATURES

New Collections provides a well-illustrated guide to all of the latest looks and trends.

Recent Collections shows the five latest collections introduced with cosy names like Easy Luxury and Chenille Tapestry.

The Bedroom Collection If you can't get to sleep at night without being perfectly co-ordinated, check out these bedlinen ranges with details of complementary cushions and lighting.

Spectrum Paint 1,350 different shades and types of mixed-to-order paint designed to co-ordinate with Sanderson wallpapers and fabrics.

Upholstered Furniture is supplied with loose covers within four to six weeks.

Made to Measure supplies not only curtains, but pelmets, tie-backs, bedheads, pillow shams, quilts, shower curtains and blinds, all within about four weeks.

Morris & Co In the autumn of 2000, Sanderson launched a range of wallpapers and fabrics inspired by the godfather of the Arts and Crafts movement, William Morris. The range includes new and recoloured designs in characteristically rich and earthy colours.

OTHER FEATURES

Brochure Request is easy to use and swift; we received our brochure within two days. Where to Find Us allows you to click on a map to find a stockist in your part of the UK.

A good site if your taste in decorating leans towards a classic, country house style but, rather like an overbearing maiden aunt, you wouldn't want to visit it more than once a season.

www.scumble-goosie.co.uk
Scumble Goosie

Overall rating: ★ ★ ★			
Classification: Company		**Readability:**	★ ★ ★
Updating: Regularly		**Content:**	★ ★ ★ ★
Navigation: ★ ★		**Speed:**	★ ★ ★ ★

UK

If you have neither the time nor the temperament to grub around in junk shops or skips to find pieces of furniture suitable for painting, the quaintly-titled Scumble Goosie provides a wide range of furniture blanks in solid wood and MDF. They can also manufacture pieces to your own specification and offer a 10 per cent discount on all items if you collect them from their base in the Cotswolds.

SPECIAL FEATURES

Selection of Products, which is also referred to as Product Range in some places, gives edited highlights from their brochure. The range covers simple, elegant pieces including Gustavian and demi-lune tables, chests of drawers, and accessories such as lamp bases, magazine racks, cache pots, and screens. Click on an image to enlarge it, or in some cases you can click beneath the image to see a painted example. Go to the Full Product List link at the bottom of the page to survey a list of their extensive collection items. There is a list here too of their range of varnishes, decoupage papers, and glazes. Unfortunately, you have to go to the Decorating Tips section to see their range of paints, or go directly to www.scumble-goosie.co.uk/paints.html.

Decorating Tips Their MDF has such a high-quality finish, it doesn't require priming so you can get straight on with the more enjoyable task of painting. This page contains clear advice on achieving a professional finish, including creating an antiqued effect using scumble glaze mixed with burnt umber acrylic paint, creating 'worn' patches on the corners to make the piece look older, and applying a crackle glaze. Click on the goose logo to see their range of Paints, a selection of handsome, subdued flat acrylics with edible names such as clotted cream, custard yellow, and rooster red.

Need It Painted? If your ideas aren't matched by your level of skill, use this facility to view their list of recommended painters across the UK. Click on the names to see a summary of their skills; people who also teach courses in paint techniques are denoted by an asterisk.

OTHER FEATURES

Latest Designs is always worth looking at to see the latest pieces the Scumble Goose has hatched up. Special Offers include many end-of-line products and also discounted pieces which have been used in television or magazine shoots. Orders are, comfortingly, delivered fully assembled so there's no tearing through the toolbox looking for exactly the right screwdriver. At the time of writing, there was no online-ordering facility although this is anticipated in the near future. At present, customers are invited to send an SAE with two first-class stamps to receive a copy of the catalogue.

A rather jumbled site which could do with some fine-tuning to do justice to Scumble Goosie's great products. It is, however, very refreshing in its encouraging tone. Have a go – you have nothing to lose but your paint.

---

www.webrugs.co.uk
Web Rugs

Overall rating: ★ ★ ★			
Classification:	Ecommerce	**Readability:**	★ ★ ★ ★
Updating:	Regularly	**Content:**	★ ★ ★ ★
Navigation:	★ ★ ★ ★	**Speed:**	★ ★ ★

UK 🔒

This dynamic young company offers 150 exclusive rug designs. The standard stock is delivered within 48 hours; out-of-stock or custom-made rugs can usually be dispatched within ten working days. The site contains lots of reassuring advice for those still nervous about ordering online, and a simple navigation menu down the left-hand-side of the page.

SPECIAL FEATURES

On-line Store allows customers to choose from Modern, Natural, Oriental, Runners, Children's, New Introductions, and Accessories. Click on the pictures to see a selection in your chosen style. In some cases you can further refine a search by clicking on a picture in these sub-menus, and a new selection of rugs in a similar colour scheme will appear. Click on the thumbnails for dimensions, pricing, and delivery details.

OTHER FEATURES

Installation Tips tells you how to get the most out of your carpet, including a recommendation on using anti-slip matting beneath the rug for safety. Care & Maintenance gives advice on vacuuming and stain removal. Rug History provides a simple introduction to their carpets. Click on a country or Rug Construction at the top of the page for more information.

An admirably clear site which shows off these affordable rugs to advantage.

OTHER SITES OF INTEREST

Clayton Munroe

www.claytonmunroe.com

Click on the smart door to enter the site of this wonderful purveyor of door furniture, stair rods, and other pieces of decorative home hardwear, and then use the menu on the left-hand side to navigate. The site shows a selection from their mail order catalogue, but choice is still extensive. Factory Shop gives directions to their showroom in South Devon, but unusually, also allows you to shop online for the latest, frequently updated factory bargains.

Curtainpole

www.curtainpole.co.uk

This small company creates attractive, reasonably-priced wrought iron curtain poles in black, antique, and polished finishes with a variety of finial designs. They are all supplied with rings, brackets, and screws so they're ready to put up as soon as they arrive. They also supply custom-made Bay Window Poles; the website gives instructions on how to measure up for a perfect fit. Delivery costs £10.50 and takes three to four weeks.

Fabric World

www.fabricworldlondon.co.uk

If you have brocade tastes and a polyester budget, Fabric World might be the answer. They run two shops in Surrey, in Sutton and Croydon, and offer a limited mail order service. They will supply a quote on most manufacturers' fabrics, the minimum order being 10 metres, and will try to better any price you have been quoted for the making-up of curtains. They supply designer fabrics which normally retail at between £30 to £50 per metre for between £10 to £20 per metre, and their own collection of hand-woven silks at £20 per metre. It's a family-run company, and they pride themselves on their free design service. They will come to your home and advise on the soft furnishings, and all you pay for is the fabric and the making-up. Go to the Interior Design page and click on the rooms to see examples of schemes they have created. The site has frequently updated special offers and customers can send an email to request samples.

Home Dec In A Sec

www.homedecinasec.com

View the range of McCalls home-decorating patterns online. Although many of the curtain styles in particular are quite elaborate, there are plenty of simpler designs to suit those whose taste or level of skill requires it. Some patterns are marked 2 Hours or Less, 90 Minute Windows, and Time-Saving Designs For People In A Hurry; click on the pattern number for an expanded view and description. This is an American site, but all of the designs are available from haberdashery departments in the UK.

Knobs & Knockers

www.knobsandknockers.co.uk

This rather nuts-and-bolts site requires quite a lot of work to find what you're looking for and doesn't really lend itself to a leisurely browse, but there are few better, more wide-ranging suppliers of door furniture, bell-pulls, and other finishing touches such as house numbers and radiator grills. Go to Search and select a Product Style from the drop-down menu, or search by product code if you have it. You can also order a catalogue by entering 1000 into the code window and clicking on the Choose a Product icon.

Linens-Online

www.linens-online.co.uk

Not the place to look for Egyptian or Sea Island cotton, but a good place to start if you're in search of bargain bedlinen and towels. Scroll down the page to find the Enter Store icon and thumbnails of their ranges will appear. Click on an appealing image and several different style options will appear. To find out about prices, click on the range that interests you. There is a good, mainstream collection, from plains to florals and geometrics. They also have a limited selection of football club towels and duvets if you have a footie fan in your family. The prices are this site's main attraction: bales of towels for £24.99, brushed cotton sheets from £8, and pretty bedspreads from £22.99.

Nono
www.nono.co.uk

Nono produces a cheerful range of fabrics and wallcoverings. Their bright colours, tempting textures, and chic neutrals add a little zip to contemporary interiors. Click on the pictures on the homepage to explore their exciting range, receive samples, and discover local stockists.

The Rug Company
www.rugcompany.co.uk

Christopher Sharp opened his first rug shop off London's King's Road in 1996 and has since created two more stores, one in Holland Park, and the other in Edinburgh. If you thought places selling exotic carpets were either too intimidatingly smart or too disconcertingly sleazy, with their constant closing down sales, then The Rug Company will appeal. Christopher Sharp's approachable attitude takes the mystique out of rug buying, and his site admirably demonstrates the sheer breadth of his range. Whether your taste is modern or traditional, you will find something here. Their stock ranges from kilims and Nepalese rugs, to classic Aubusson, Zeigler, and Caucasian carpets. Now, they can even produce a rug to your specification in any design, colour and style made with fine quality hand-spun wool and silk. You can even arrange to take a rug home with you to see how it looks. The site gives a good introduction to the comprehensive range, although it is a little slow as it is so heavily illustrated. Choose to view by rug type or by rugs in interiors.

Tapisserie
www.tapisserie.co.uk

If needlepoint is your passion, then this site will become a firm favourite. Tapisserie was created by Lady Palumbo in 1986, and today, her jewel box of a shop is crammed with beautiful cushions, rugs, chairs, and even handbags and slippers, all worked in exquisite needlepoint. Click on the picture of the Chelsea shop to enter the site. Of particular interest is the Bespoke service. Tapisserie's designers will create hand-painted canvases, designed to fit your piece of furniture, using your fabrics, magazine clippings or photographs as inspiration. They can also look at a picture of your piece and suggest designs from their extensive range that could be suitably adapted. If you have more imagination than skill, then join the Alice-banded set at one of Hilda Sheppard's popular and enjoyable Wednesday morning Needlework Classes. Prices are not cheap, but the range and level of finish is unrivalled.

Wallflowers' Home Decorating Projects and Ideas
www.wallflowers.net

An American site that contains regularly updated features on running up your own home furnishings. Emphasis is on simple projects which won't break the bank and don't require a City & Guilds' Certificate in upholstery to complete. Use the menu on the left-hand side of the page to browse through the various categories. The photography is not good and reflects the rather 'enthusiastic amateur' nature of this site, but instructions are clear and simple to follow.

The World of Interiors Design Studio
www.thedesignstudio.com

A site created by the good people at the madly chic magazine to help us create our own schemes and swatch boards. Click on the computer screen logo to enter the directory of fabric and wallpaper, and register to start browsing through the hundreds of designs. Use the menu to select a colour, type of fabric or paper, and a designer, and press Search to discover materials that match your criteria. A little slow, but good fun nonetheless.

Chapter 03

shopping

Could it be more simple? Imagine doing your Christmas shopping in your pyjamas, lifting nothing more strenuous than a cup of coffee, with no struggling through busy streets lugging arm-extending packages. Or picking out the perfect birthday gift which you don't even have to wrap yourself. Or putting the perfect finishing touches to your sitting room without having to trek halfway across town to do so.

Of course, it's not always so simple. Delivery charges and times, complicated return policies, and items which don't look quite as heavenly in your home as they did on the website are just some of the pitfalls of ordering online. The

best companies, however, are realising that when we order online, we do not expect the same level of service as we get on the high street; we expect it to be even better.

Reviews in this chapter are generally shorter than in some of the others. This is not because the sites here have less to offer. Rather, it is because there are so many companies now who offer good online shopping services that we chose to give you a taster of the many rather than expansive details of the few. You're bound to find something to thrill you here, whether your taste is Ron Arad modern or English Country House traditional. Enjoy.

www.homeelements.co.uk
Home Elements Ltd

Overall rating: ★ ★ ★ ★			
Classification: Ecommerce		**Readability:**	★ ★ ★ ★
Updating: Seasonally		**Content:**	★ ★ ★ ★ ★
Navigation: ★ ★ ★ ★		**Speed:**	★ ★ ★ ★

UK 🔒

Home Elements describe themselves as 'mail-order shopping, Twenty-First Century style', and they certainly offer some of the most exciting online merchandise around. Many of the original and inspirational items are unique to them and many come from up-and-coming British designers.

SPECIAL FEATURES

Sensual Living is a feast of mohair blankets, hand-spun vases, and made-to-order contemporary pottery. Click on the images for more details and an enlarged picture of the piece.

Café Society is the place to stop, over your café au lait, if you're set on giving your kitchen the ambience of a French bistro. Look out for chrome Straw Dispensers, Paris salt and pepper shakers, and lovely, hand-finished Carte du Jour tableware.

Kids at Home will be a disappointment if you think children's things should come in insipid pink, blue, or lemon. Bright blankets, pretty china, clothes hangers in the shape of animals, and silver christening spoons are all unusual and attractive.

Kitchen Essentials is full of well-designed bargains. The Basic Stacking glasses start at an incredible £7 for a set of six water glasses.

OTHER FEATURES

If you're looking for an unusual gift for a magpie-eyed friend, look at Shine On for lots of sparkly accessories. Silver coloured spectacle cases, letter openers, storage pots, tape measures, and travel clocks are particularly covetable.

A well-designed site packed with refreshing, modern and elegant objects for the home.

www.lakeland.co.uk

Lakeland Limited

Overall rating: ★ ★ ★ ★ ★			
Classification:	Ecommerce	**Readability:**	★ ★ ★ ★ ★
Updating:	Seasonally	**Content:**	★ ★ ★ ★ ★
Navigation:	★ ★ ★ ★	**Speed:**	★ ★ ★ ★

UK

When feed salesman Alan Rayner and his wife Dorothy started selling plastic bags from a market stall 35 years ago, they couldn't have imagined how big their business would become. Today, their three sons mastermind a company which sells 1,500 different products, sends out a million catalogues a year, has 21 stores from Aberdeen to Truro and mails 5,000 carefully-packed parcels every day. Log on to the site and the Product of the Day appears in a pop-up window. If you have a paper catalogue, key the reference number into the Product Search box on the lower right-hand side. If you want to browse, look through the sections under Online Shopping on the right-hand side. When you find something to interest you, click on the thumbnail to see an enlarged image. It's a wonderful, easy-to-use site, but it's almost a shame to shop online. Regular customers will miss being gently talked through their order in friendly Cumbrian tones by the company's exemplary staff.

SPECIAL FEATURES

Kitchenware covers 24 categories, including three staples of traditional British life: Baking Day, The Great British Roast, and Bargains. If you're the thrifty type, you'll buy your barbecue equipment, citronella candles, and garden torches in the autumn when they're a steal.

Delia's Collection When the Queen of Home-Cooking blesses a piece of equipment with her approval, kitchen departments across the country brace themselves for the rush. Avoid the crush yourself and view her 45 special items here, from Pure Iranian Saffron, to the Olive Wood Lemon Reamer, her perfect Omelette Pan and, of course, her books. In fact, practically the only thing they don't sell are the white eggs she made so popular when they appeared on her book's dust jackets.

Storage Solutions is a godsend for those of us have too much stuff and not enough places to put it. It is divided into 25 categories, including Laundry Made Easy, Wood & Wicker Baskets, Home Office, Keep It In The Car, and lots of cleaning products which are exclusive to them.

OTHER FEATURES

Make the festive season less stressful by ordering essentials online. Lakeland seems to have everything but the turkey in their Ideas for Christmas section; In Preparation includes delicious things such as Taylor's Brandy Butter, Organic Wild Cranberry Sauce, and Fig Balsamic Vinegar.

A wonderful site from a company which seems to take its exponential growth in its stride – without losing its characteristic commitment to customer service and innovative, practical products.

www.emccord.com
McCord Online

Overall rating: ★ ★ ★ ★			
Classification: Ecommerce		**Readability:**	★ ★ ★ ★ ★
Updating: Varies		**Content:**	★ ★ ★ ★ ★
Navigation: ★ ★ ★ ★		**Speed:**	★ ★ ★ ★

UK

McCord's emphasis is on comfort, versatility and great design; their aim, to create 'inspirational, well-crafted furnishings that both look good and work hard'. This is furniture for grown-up, self-confident houses that aren't afraid of the odd touch of whimsy. Use the menu down the left-hand side to move between merchandise sections, or use the menu bar at the top of the page for more practical information on ordering.

SPECIAL FEATURES

Living This section is divided into Furniture, Textiles, Accessories, and Upholstery. Look out for the great selection of sofas and chairs, many of which come in 17 choices of fabric, and don't miss the irresistible Manhattan Collection in delicious, soft brown leather. Accessories includes many original gifts, including firescreens, wine racks, and candlesticks.

Kids' Stuff is almost too good to leave to the small people. Funky alarm clocks, traditional toys, and zippy bedlinen are all well designed and durable. One highlight is the Starspangled quilt which is very Ralph Lauren at a fraction of the price.

OTHER FEATURES

Don't miss **Textiles**, with its fantastic faux-fur bean bags, destined to bring out the well-heeled hippy in the most buttoned-up of souls. Gifts & Ideas is particularly good for Seasonal Gifts which are shot in a very 'It's A Wonderful Life' fashion, though what James Stewart would have made of the Fibre Optic Reindeer is anyone's guess.

Great products, beautifully shot, on a wonderfully accessible site. Whether your taste is cool and urban, or American country, there is plenty of great stuff here.

www.okadirect.com
OKA Direct

Overall rating: ★ ★ ★ ★ ★			
Classification:	Ecommerce	**Readability:**	★ ★ ★ ★
Updating:	Varies	**Content:**	★ ★ ★ ★ ★
Navigation:	★ ★ ★ ★	**Speed:**	★ ★ ★ ★

UK

This catalogue oozes class and self-assured charm. The three directors bring their diverse talents to creating a wonderful site: Annabel Astor is a respected interior designer and former jewellery maker; Sue Jones worked for Jasper Conran for ten years; and Lucinda Waterhouse is an inspired floral designer. In a relatively short period of time, they have created a company which is now a byword for elegance. Use the menu across the top of the page to move around the site.

SPECIAL FEATURES

Our Collection gives a detailed introduction to the OKA 'look'. Use the drop-down menu to go to different sections. Eastern Aesthetics highlights the Kyoto range of pared-down oriental pieces which would slip easily into any traditional English interior or look quite at home in a city loft. Urban Chic is full of pieces that could add a little warmth to a cool, urban interior. Look at Delusions of Grandeur for the fabulous finishing touches any well-dressed scheme needs. And if your best friend really is your dog, go to Pet Power to view the magisterial Manhattan dog bed with its own elegant fleece cushion.

Rooms Items from the other sections are divided here by their suitability for particular rooms. Don't miss Entertaining for its lovely icebuckets, tray tables, and trays. They would even turn dinner in front of the television into an event.

OTHER FEATURES

Refine your Search under Present Finder, Keyword Search, or Browse our Collection. Your Shopping provides a fast-track ordering system. If you have a catalogue, all you need to do is put the order code into the box provided. Click on the top left-hand side of the screen to order a free OKA catalogue.

The beautiful photography on this site makes it all too easy to imagine the stylish objects in your own home. How did we ever live without those beautiful Indochine rattan chests?

www.bluedeco.com

BLUEdeco.com

Overall rating: ★ ★ ★ ★			
Classification: Ecommerce		**Readability:**	★ ★ ★ ★
Updating: Regularly		**Content:**	★ ★ ★ ★ ★
Navigation: ★ ★ ★ ★		**Speed:**	★ ★ ★

UK

This young company offers the best of British design online. When you get to the stylish homepage, roll the cursor over the images to reveal the section to which it pertains. It's just as good for exquisite, small gifts as it is for large pieces of furniture. You'll be torn between wanting to tell all of your smartest friends about this company and keeping it to yourself. They have a cunning scheme whereby you earn a 20 per cent referral fee on products bought from the site by people you have recommended.

SPECIAL FEATURES

Furniture Look here for exquisite chairs, stools, and tables. When they come in different woods or finishes, use the drop-down menu to define your choice. If you find something you like, there is sometimes a link to the designer's website.

Tableware If your table's looking tired, bring it into the Twenty-First Century with covetable accessories. This page includes that most rare of items: the chic tablemat. It's only a shame they are not heatproof. Look out for beautiful Wooden Bowls, Bullet Vases, and the stunning Pewter Coffee Presses.

OTHER FEATURES

Don't forget to check out Ceramics, Glassware, and Metalwork for myriad modern must-haves.

An elegant site full of carefully chosen, beautifully made British design. It'll have you phoning your credit card company and begging for a hike in your limit.

www.thecube.uk.com
The Cube Collection

Overall rating: ★ ★ ★ ★			
Classification:	Ecommerce	Readability:	★ ★ ★
Updating:	Regularly	Content:	★ ★ ★ ★ ★
Navigation:	★ ★ ★	Speed:	★ ★ ★

UK 🔒

www.divertimenti.co.uk
Divertimenti

Overall rating: ★ ★ ★ ★			
Classification:	Ecommerce	Readability:	★ ★ ★ ★
Updating:	Seasonally	Content:	★ ★ ★ ★ ★
Navigation:	★ ★ ★ ★	Speed:	★ ★ ★

UK 🔒

The remarkably lovely and original pieces to be found in The Cube Collection exude a quiet glamour. Their slogan is where 'Luxury meets Purity', and for once, the merchandise lives up to the PR. Click on the menu at the bottom of the page to move around between sections.

SPECIAL FEATURES

Online Catalogue The Cube Room Collection is divided into Living Room, Dining Room, and Bedroom. Click on the room to see a larger picture but not, unfortunately, any details of the merchandise displayed. You need to trawl through the rest of the catalogue for that which, due to the beauty of the pieces, is no great shame. The Cube Furniture Range is an essay in elegance, with satisfying square shapes and luxurious finishes such as linen and nubuck. The Cube Invisible Range is a fabulous collection of Plexiglas furniture, from simple trays to 'invisible' console and side tables. These are perfect for the contemporary interior and, with care, can work very well in more traditional interiors too. The Cube Window Range is wonderfully original, with curtain poles made from bamboo and perspex and divine pashmina panel curtains.

An almost unspeakably lovely site crammed with objects of desire. It's just a shame that you have to trawl through the whole catalogue to locate information on the pieces used in the room shots.

Since they opened their first shop in 1963, Divertimenti has been one of the best sources for professional-quality cooking equipment and beautiful hand-made tableware. Their site is very simple to navigate. Use Search for a Product on the left-hand-side and refine your search by keyword, category and price range. On all pages, click on Here to browse or use the drop-down Select a Category box to go to an area in which you are specifically interested.

SPECIAL FEATURES

Divertimenti Collection comprises 34 pages of the company's core range, from the fabulously glamorous brushed metal Soda Syphon, to possibly the best garlic press in the world ever, their Good Grips press.

Cookware from Delia's Series Divertimenti's association with Delia Smith goes back to the 1970s, when most of us still thought a tagine was a dance step. Look here for equipment from her television series, from the great-looking nutmeg grater, to the virtually indestructible SKK pots and pans.

Essentials Collection is finely honed from years of selling high-quality cookware. For products that look good and work hard, their selection is exemplary. Look out for the party-size lasagna dishes, fiendish poultry shears, and Sabatier carving knives that are robust enough to last through a lifetime of carving roasts, paring vegetables, and peeling fruit.

Mediterranean Collection is one of Divertimenti's signature looks, indeed they were one of the first companies to introduce this kind of brightly-coloured pottery to the UK. Provençal blue and green tableware is justifiably a classic, and the best part of it is that it's dishwasher-safe. The Solimene range in bright yellow, blue, and a pinkish-red is cheerful enough to make you rediscover breakfast as a lifestyle choice. And it's so much easier buying it from Divertimenti than cramming it into your carry-on luggage.

OTHER FEATURES

The easiest place to find a present for a foodie is in their Gift Collection. Don't miss the Daube pot, Pentola paella pans, and the distinctive Square poet plates.

An impressively comprehensive site with everything the keen cook might ever need. From preparation, to oven, to table, it's all here.

www.handbag.com/shopping/home_garden
Handbag.com

Overall rating: ★ ★ ★ ★			
Classification:	Ecommerce	**Readability:**	★ ★ ★ ★
Updating:	Regularly	**Content:**	★ ★ ★ ★
Navigation:	★ ★ ★ ★	**Speed:**	★ ★ ★ ★

UK

This is a comprehensive and rigorous site which provides a great survey of current online home shopping. There are plenty of special offers which appear in a pop-up window with, helpfully, other related areas of interest. Go to the left-hand side of the screen to scan down the What to Find Where menu, and go to the right-hand side to view current features.

SPECIAL FEATURES

Shop Review gives a great survey of some of the best home shopping sites on the web, with information on delivery times and costs.

Now Read This contains good features on shopping. Let them scour the web for you to bring you the very best.

Our Shopping Promise indicates just how thorough their screening is. They've bought from every store they recommend, and only feature etailers who handle your credit card securely and keep your details private. They must also have a clear returns policy and offer proper customer support, either by email or over the telephone.

OTHER FEATURES

If you're searching for a present and are low on inspiration, go to the Gift Selector and use the drop-down Select a Gift menu for a list of choices.

want to read **more reviews** on this subject?

log on to **www.thegoodwebguide.co.uk**

Handbag.com is one of the best sites on the web if your credit card is burning a hole in your wallet. There is an expansive choice of clearly laid-out home merchandise so you're bound to find something to suit you.

www.theholdingcompany.co.uk

The Holding Company

Overall rating: ★ ★ ★ ★			
Classification:	Ecommerce	**Readability:**	★ ★ ★ ★
Updating:	Regularly	**Content:**	★ ★ ★ ★
Navigation:	★ ★ ★ ★ ★	**Speed:**	★ ★ ★

If your home is more haphazard than haven-like, and your mornings are stress-fests of hunting for car keys and matching socks, let The Holding Company come to the rescue. Their organisational tools, previously accessible only to those who could visit their store on London's King's Road or had a copy of their attractive paper catalogue, are now available to all of us via the internet. Click on the logo to enter the site, and scan the menu down the left-hand side. If you're still baffled, click on Help! for advice on navigating the site, but you really shouldn't need it. It is, fittingly, simplicity itself to use.

SPECIAL FEATURES

Catalogue In her opening letter, the Company's dynamic American founder, Dawna Walter, tells us 'we strive to provide you with essential products that we feel will improve the quality of your life, giving you the freedom to enjoy the time saved by being organised'. You may view this with characteristic Anglo-Saxon scepticism until you look down the page. Perhaps the folding screen with woven seagrass in bamboo would help you to conceal your home office, the video tower in media storage would prevent your flat from looking like a recently-broken-into Blockbuster store, and the large embroidered toy bag in kids' accessories would look better in your sitting room than the Kilimanjaro of Lego which resides there presently.

OTHER FEATURES

Special Offers are regularly updated, if a little limited at the time of writing. Mailing List allows you either to register to receive emails about specific offers, events, and new products, or to order a paper catalogue. If you like it all so much you want to join the company, click on Employment Opportunities. Our Shop takes you to a page containing directions to the store and opening hours.

A suitably well-organised site from the home organisation company. Their shoe holders, sweater boxes, and cable tidys might not change your life, but they may make it more manageable.

www.housemailorder.co.uk
Hambledon Gallery

Overall rating: ★ ★ ★ ★			
Classification:	Ecommerce	**Readability:**	★ ★
Updating:	Infrequently	**Content:**	★ ★ ★ ★ ★
Navigation:	★ ★ ★ ★	**Speed:**	★ ★ ★

UK 🔒

This is the online mail-order service of Winchester's Hambledon Gallery, which specialises in smart accessories and small pieces of furniture in sensuous materials like rattan, soapstone, and mother-of-pearl. It's a fresh, modern site that manages to maintain its cool without being chilly. There is limited product description, but it is beautifully illustrated with the kind of simple, yet incredibly chic, photographs we associate with upmarket interior design magazines.

Use the menu at the bottom of the inviting homepage, which is divided into rooms. The one drawback of this site is that there is no way of knowing what items are in stock or prospective delivery times. Their motto may be 'carpe diem, and all that', but it's a shame no one seized the day to update the introduction to the homepage. At the time of writing, it was six months out of date, which does not inspire confidence.

SPECIAL FEATURES

Sitting Room The stylish merchandise presented here is great value and so well selected that you murmur to yourself, 'I've been looking for one of those', with every new page. Huge rattan log baskets start at £39.95, and you could add a little eastern promise to your living room with a great pair of bamboo tables at only £39.95.

Dining Room The pieces here could transform mealtimes from mundane to magnificent, with wonderful soapstone dishes and plates, mother-of-pearl spoons, and salt and pepper shakers, and striking wooden table lights.

Nursery If you're looking for a cot blanket that shrieks Milan rather than Mothercare, this is the place to look. There are also adorable newborn booties for £9.95, and a small rag rug, a steal at £9.95, which would look just as good in the bathroom as in the nursery.

It may be a magazine stylist's idea of nirvana, but the rest of us could do with a little more information on products, delivery times, returns, and exchanges.

www.next.co.uk
Next

Overall rating: ★ ★ ★ ★			
Classification:	Ecommerce	**Readability:**	★ ★ ★ ★ ★
Updating:	Seasonally	**Content:**	★ ★ ★ ★
Navigation:	★ ★ ★ ★ ★	**Speed:**	★ ★ ★ ★

UK

Many of Next's contemporary, value-for-money products are now available online via their swift, easy-to-navigate site. Click on Homewares at the top of the homepage to view the range, then click on the thumbnails to see more details about each item. You can also Order a Catalogue, which will enable you to use the Quick Shop facility by simply entering in the product number. On many of the pieces, you can expect next-day delivery and free returns if they aren't suitable.

SPECIAL FEATURES

Cushions & Throws includes scented cushions at £15.99, heart-shaped pillows in animal prints for £16.99, and you can even take a tiger to bed with you in the shape of the faux-tiger-skin hotwater bottle cover.

Curtains & Accessories If you're a stranger to the sewing machine, let Next take care of it for you with their smart range of ready-made curtains. There are plenty of bold colours, neutrals, and accessories such as the bay-window curtain pole and pretty hold-backs.

Rugs can transform the look of a room. Next's collection is bright and contemporary; the Square on Square runner, £69.99, and the Circle rug, £39.99, are particularly striking.

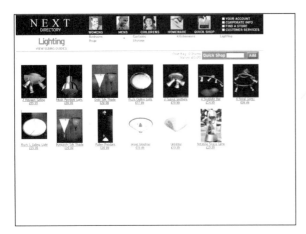

OTHER FEATURES

Accessories & Gifts includes many inexpensive small pieces, even lovely bouquets of flowers. Laundry could make washday less of a chore with brightly coloured clothes bins and baskets.

Great colours, great shapes, and good prices on a well-designed site which is simplicity itself to use.

www.cucinadirect.co.uk
Cucina Direct

Overall rating: ★ ★ ★			
Classification:	Ecommerce	**Readability:**	★ ★ ★ ★
Updating:	Varies	**Content:**	★ ★ ★ ★ ★
Navigation:	★ ★ ★	**Speed:**	★ ★

UK 🔒

The company claims that this is the site for people who love to cook, but they could have legitimately added to that those who love to entertain, or simply love to eat. They stock a wonderful range of simple, elegant products for the kitchen and dining room which are as practical as they are beautiful. Go to the pretty homepage and click on the thumbnails to browse through the sections, or use the menu at the bottom of the page. Click on Browse by Theme and a menu will appear down the left-hand side of the page which includes such tempting sections as Formal Dining, Professional Pans, and Old Favourites. Our only quibble with this site is that it is frustratingly slow to load the different pages, which spoils what is otherwise a pleasurable experience.

SPECIAL FEATURES

Cooking Equipment includes everything you need to create a well-equipped kitchen. Use the menu down the left-hand side for a specific search, or meander through the selected merchandise which appears in the middle of the page.

Electrical Appliances Carefully selected ice-cream makers, Dualit toasters and kettles, and stainless-steel breadmakers, in fact everything that the well-dressed kitchen deserves.

Household does its very best to make cleaning seem like an aesthetic experience. Cape Cod polishing cloths, lavender

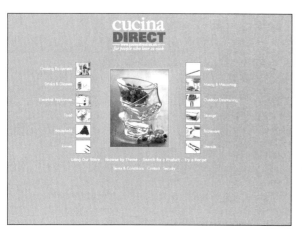

and verbena linen water for the iron, ostrich feather dusters, and the traditional dustpan and brush in stainless steel are almost too good looking to be consigned to the cupboard under the sink.

OTHER FEATURES

You can Search for a Product using a code number, name, or description to cut down on browsing time. Those who have enjoyed the delicious recipes that Cucina include in their paper catalogue don't have to miss out on them here. Try a Recipe includes such delicacies as wild mushroom risotto, potato-courgette frittata, and plum and cinnamon ice cream.

Keen cooks will visit this site often. Let's hope they can speed it up a little. It's so slow I almost lost the will to shop.

OTHER SITES OF INTEREST

Alba Tops
www.albatops.co.uk
If your new kitchen is going to come in for heavy-duty use, then you might want to consider one of Alba Tops' worksurfaces, which come in Corian, Granite, Stainless Steel, Hardwood and Laminate. They'll sell you a fixed length, or cut it to a template if you prefer.

Art Room
www.artroom.com
If museum-quality antiques are a little out of your reach, then The Art Room could provide a solution. They sell replicas and reproductions of pieces from some of the world's finest museums and collections, in many cases scaled to suit the modern home. Go to the menu down the left-hand side and use the drop-down menu to Pick a Section. Choose from European, Victorian, Art Nouveau and Deco, Impressionists, Contemporary, World, and Ancient. Of course, you could go for your very own copy of the Gozzoli Wall Hanging from the Medici-Riccardi Palace in Florence, or you could try one of their more whimsical pieces, such as the Cocteau Cat T-Shirt or the divine Little Angel baby's romper suit complete with matching winged booties. Order online via a secure server.

The Chair Company
www.thechair.co.uk
The Chair Company stock over 100 contemporary chairs in their Fulham and Battersea showrooms, but they take orders over the telephone for the many smart chairs illustrated on their website. Enter the site and click on an image to see all of that range of chairs, from solid wood, to plastic, folding numbers and stools. They also stock a limited range of tables, from pale wood, to chrome and glass. This is a lovely-looking site which offers admirable choice.

Chiasmus
www.chiasmus.co.uk
This site could be better designed, but it's worth a visit for the fresh and funky products it contains. Our Products contains everything from greetings cards, candles, yoghurt body lotion, and wonderfully chic short rock ice glasses. This is a great place to look if you're stuck on a gift for a difficult-to-buy-for twentysomething with a yearning for kitsch.

Click Deco
www.clickdeco.com
This is a great site for fun, funky, kitsch-y accessories. They're cheap and almost pathalogically cheerful. You just didn't know where to look for that ceramic Buddha money box, Hawaiian fabric flower curtain, or teddy bear lamp? The answer is here. Unfortunately, the form used to enter your credit card details is not secure. Although Click Deco claims that information is sent securely, you have no way of being certain.

Codygifts.com
www.codygifts.com
If Christmas and birthdays fill you with terror, take advantage of your own personal shopping service which allows you to select a gift by Occasion, Personality, Gender, and Price. Gift Emergency on the left-hand side of the page is a godsend for the forgetful. Order a present by four in the afternoon, and it will be delivered the next day.

Contemporary Living
www.contemporaryliving.com
A great place to look for contemporary products for the home, all sourced from British, German, and Danish manufacturers. The selection is limited, but demonstrates a good eye for contemporary styling. Use the menu down the left-hand side of the site to navigate between sections. Crazy for Coffee has some wonderful cafetieres, cups, and vacuum jugs; Tea Time brings an old tradition up to date with modern teapots and tea glasses. Stylish to Serve has smart table accessories such as the Salad Tongs, Carving Set, and the Cheese Dome. Clivingmag provides a brief stop-over for those 'pursuing a modern lifestyle', with news on travel, contemporary design shows, and home features.

The Dining Chair Company
www.diningchair.co.uk
Interior designers Tricia Fallon and Alison Jackson set up this company after experiencing difficulty sourcing good-looking, comfortable chairs for their clients. Click on the row of handsome chairs at the bottom of the page to view more details about each piece. There is wonderful attention to detail, with customers being able to select the stain used on the chair legs, and the fabric and trimmings used. They aren't cheap, but consider how much time you spend at the dining table in a lifetime, and they suddenly don't seem so expensive.

Europe By Net
www.europebynet.com
Top-end fixtures and furnishings from all over Europe at extremely competitive prices. The range is exclusive (or very small, depending on how you look at it) and is biased towards the ornate, with chandeliers aplenty in the lighting section.

Furniture123
www.furniture123.com
A vast, online furniture store, which aims to undercut highstreet prices by sidestepping high rentals, and presenting its goods in cyberspace. The range is decidedly middle of the road, but there is plenty to choose from. You can order free colour swatches to help with your choice, but since the photos can be misleading, it's perhaps best used as a discount catalogue, for items you've seen in the high street, but want to get cheaper.

The General Trading Company

www.general-trading.co.uk

This site gives an introduction to the products available at the smart Sloane Square store. They display an eclectic range of traditional and contemporary pieces with considerable panache. There is no online ordering yet, but you can order a paper catalogue from the site, as well as keep up to date with special events and sales.

Haf Designs

www.hafdesigns.co.uk

If your door handles and light switches are ruining your chic modern scheme, introduce yourself to Haf Designs' smart stainless steel finishing touches in sleek shapes. Click on Bathrooms, Essentials, Door Furniture, and Electrical to view the product range and buy their products online via a secure server.

Hilary's Blinds

www.web-blinds.com

If you are one of those people who are driven to distraction in the quest to find blinds that are just so, Hilary's Blinds may be just the answer. Blinds are made to measure, via an easy five-step ordering plan, and a free swatch-sampling service to help make your choice. However, they rely on you to take an accurate set of measurements.

Inhabit

www.inhabit.co.uk

This is a bright, youthful site which promises 'interior shopping for a new generation'. Choice is limited, but it's lots of fun and the prices are great. Merchandise is divided into Colour Crazy, Contemporary Chic, Kitsch Cool, and Cult Classics. Expect lots of funky plastics, brushed metal, chrome, and cheerful candles.

In-Sinks

www.in-sinks.com

A range of kitchen sinks, taps, water filters and waste disposal units supplied by such diverse brands as Royal Doulton to Smeg. The homepage is divided by brands, so it can be a pain to search, though it's worth the extra effort, as the prices are often lower than those in the hight street.

Interior Internet

www.interiorinternet

Interior Internet manages to successfully provide a wide range of interior furnishings and still maintain a highly selective design ethos. It's a portal signed aimed primarily at the interior design industry (with some items imported specially to order) so it's for serious interior decoration enthusiasts only.

Intersaver

www.intersaver.com

Intersaver offers plenty of domestic appliances if you're looking for nothing more than a popular brand at a discounted price. There's a substantial range, which you can look through by clicking on one of the icons, such as Sound, Vision and Home Office, or Domestic Appliances. There's also plenty of information on model specifications such as capacity and temperature control, so unlike many other discount sites, you don't need to go have a look at them in a shop first.

The Iron-Bed Company

www.ironbed.com

This site is an extension of the mail-order company, which has been run by the Notley family since 1994. There's a diverse selection of hand-made wrought Iron beds, from Gothic to Ultra-slick modern.

John Lewis

www.johnlewis.com

This large department store chain is dipping its toe cautiously into the choppy waters of etail with a limited selection of plain towels, decorative towels, beach towels, bath robes and bath mats. Roll the cursor over the logo on the top left-hand side of the homepage, go to Shopping, and then click on Home. Gift wrapping is available and you can choose between standard and express delivery.

Kode
www.kodelighting.co.uk
This London-based company specialises in stylish, modern lighting and is named after the first product it manufactured. Click on (2) at the bottom of the page to introduce yourself to their inspired, elegant designs. You can't order online, but you can buy over the phone using a credit card.

Leslie Geddes-Brown's Online Shopping and Mail Order Made Easy
www.lesliegeddesbrown.com
Entering the website of style, shopping, and gardening journalist Leslie Geddes-Browne feels like being let in on a wonderful secret. She shares with us an address book built up over years of successful style sleuthing, along with Regular Features and an excellent Home Shopping Adviser which allows you to search for retailers using a keyword. Use the menu down the left-hand side of the site to go to General Catalogues, House & Garden, Beauty & Luxuries, Presents, Celebrations, and many others. Ask Leslie allows you to get advice from the guru herself on almost anything relating to the home and garden. One visit and you will be adding this site to your favourites list quicker than you can say 'Charge it!'.

Liberty
www.liberty-of-london.com
If you can't visit the Regent Street store but need a quick style fix, this site provides a well-chosen selection of desirable Liberty merchandise. Click on For the Home in the menu at the top of the homepage and select from Bath, Bedroom, Candles & Holders, Dining, Frames & Albums, Kitchen, and Vases. You can buy online via a secure server and, in certain areas, you can search by your postcode to see if evening or Saturday delivery is available.

Maelstrom
www.maelstrom.co.uk
This cool, urban site is like top-shelf material for the Tate Modern brigade. Ron Arad, Philippe Starck, and Charles and Ray Eames, are just some of the designers whose pieces are generously illustrated on this speedy site. There are regular competitions to win free pieces, with questions on the designers' lives, just to make sure you're sitting up straight in that Le Corbusier chair and paying attention. One of the most compelling sections is Urban Life – the VIP Ashtrays in wine-gum colours are fabulous enough to make you want to rip off your nicotine patch and hi-tail it to the newsagent on your Mathmos MicroSkate Scooter.

Noel Hennessy Furniture
www.noelhennessy.com
Mr Hennessy's London showroom is known for its friendly, unstuffy approach to selling contemporary European furniture, and this attitude is reflected in his chic and cheerful website. The Collection in the menu bar at the top of the page leads you through Living Room, Dining Room, Bedroom, Home Office, Lighting and Rugs. There is a limited selection of products available online at the moment, but nonetheless this is a wonderful site to visit.

Ocean
www.oceancatalogue.com
From the Style File homepage, click on the drop-down menu on the left to Pick a Room, then click on thumbnails to get details. Imaginative furnishings come in super sexy cowhide, bamboo and linen. All very stylish, and great prices too. Bargains contains real discounts of sometimes up to 50 per cent and Best Sellers is home to the Stapleless Stapler, Spiral Paper Clips, and a wonderful bed made from beech. The children's toys are fabulous too, particularly the Architect Building Sets, from £29.95, which comprises real, fired mini-bricks, red pantiles, and convincing potato starch mortar.

Purves & Purves
www.purves.co.uk

This store on London's Tottenham Court Road has made its name from innovative, modern design, and old-fashioned customer service. The Products section includes furniture from Ron Arad, Philippe Starck, and Matthew Hilton, as well as pieces by new, up-and-coming designers. Click on Living Room, Dining Room, Bedroom, or Office to view the products. Funky couples can use their Wedding List service. Use the Wish List to search for an unusual gift. Fill in your details and a description of the person you're buying for and an indication of your budget, and they will email you with their suggestion.

Small Island Trader
www.smallisland.demon.co.uk

This is a wonderful place to buy high-quality china and crystal online. Small Island is run by a British/American couple who live in the heart of the Potteries, making them ideally placed to dispatch Spode, Wedgwood, and Royal Doulton. Their range is not just limited to Staffordshire, however, as they sell designs from all the major British and many European manufacturers. They also have a Bridal Gift Service and Cookshop section. Crystal includes pieces from Waterford and Stuart. All of their pieces are perfect, no seconds here, and delivery within the UK is a flat rate of £7.95 however much you order. Prices are quoted without VAT, but despite that they are reasonable. The couple call themselves 'digital shopkeepers', and an old-fashioned commitment to customer service is reflected in their high-tech operation.

Stylesource
www.stylesource.co.uk

This is a fantastic, friendly site with constantly updated material and an address book that is second to none. Go to the homepage and click on Design & Decor for lots of inspiration and to enter the Shop section. Use the menu down the right-hand side of the page to select your area of interest. If you're a real home bird, you'll love their Cuisine, DIY and Garden sections too.

This is Furniture
www.thisisfurniture.com

Though the homepage is more high street than high fashion, the goods on offer are stylish and contemporary. The selection is modest, but if you want ultra-modern simplicity then there's plenty to choose from. You'll need to order over the phone, as there's presently no secure server.

TimeOut.com
www.timeout.com

If you live in London, or are planning a visit, Time Out magazine's website is a mine of information. Click on London Shopping for all of the latest on new shops, new products, and new trends. Use the menu down the left-hand side of the page to find out about all of the best auctions, department stores, markets, and much, much more.

want to read **more reviews** on this subject?

log on to

www.thegoodwebguide.co.uk

Chapter 04

ezines and newsletters

There are many familiar titles in this section on ezines, but almost exclusively they refer to the American magazines bearing the same name. It is disappointing that, with a couple of notable exceptions, British interiors magazines don't share the dynamic attitude of their American sisters. Disappointingly, they often fail to grasp the opportunities that the internet offers. Do a search for your favourite title and chances are that you'll turn up nothing more riveting than an advertisers' rate card and information on subscribing. This all seems a little mean, as though by extending a more generous service to online readers they would ensure we won't pick up their magazines at the news-stands. We look forward to the day when they recognise internet sites as a great way of giving their extensive archives of features a prolonged life and creating greater brand loyalty. If the numerous La Mags can do it, why not their well-upholstered stable mates?

www.allthatwomenwant.com
All That Women Want

Overall rating: ★ ★ ★ ★ ★			
Classification:	Ezine	Readability:	★ ★ ★ ★
Updating:	Monthly	Content:	★ ★ ★ ★ ★
Navigation:	★ ★ ★ ★	Speed:	★ ★ ★

(US)

Nothing to do with the downmarket clothing store that shares its name, All That Women Want is a wide-ranging monthly ezine, covering parenting, work, organising, and home. The text on the homepage may be a blazing Schiaparelli pink, but it's not at all fluffy. Use the menu at the top of the page to search between sections, or use the contents list down the right-hand side of the page to view this month's features. The left-hand side also shows the highlighted features in each section. The site has some of the best links on the web for the domestically inclined – you can even treat yourself to a daily horoscope to see if the stars are in alignment to tackle that paint finish successfully. Domestic Goddesses can subscribe to their monthly newsletter.

SPECIAL FEATURES

House & Home points to some of the best decorating, home maintenance, and gardening sites on the net and, although this is an American site, many of the links are British. Particularly good are 123 Sort-It for the congenitally cluttered, and Learn2.com, a site which gives clear and simple instructions on doing everything from slicing an onion to repairing a scratched CD. Links open up in a separate window.

Antiques & Collectibles gives advice on bidding for pieces online, and reviews of recommended sites covering a wide range of topics from creating a collection, to caring for treasured items.

Packed with information, bright and accessible, All That Women Want gives access to some of the best information on the web, and provides a welcome short cut to endless trawling.

have you registered for free updates?

log on to

www.thegoodwebguide.co.uk

www.bhglive.com
Better Homes & Gardens

Overall rating: ★ ★ ★ ★			
Classification:	Ezine	Readability:	★ ★ ★ ★ ★
Updating:	Monthly	Content:	★ ★ ★ ★ ★
Navigation:	★ ★ ★ ★	Speed:	★ ★ ★

US

The American magazine Better Homes & Gardens makes great use of its wealth of archived features in the creation of this site. It's bright, very accessible, and, after half an hour browsing, the chances are you'll find their 'have a go' attitude infectious. Whether you're interested in cooking, decorating, or gardening, use the menu bar at the top of the screen to move between sections.

SPECIAL FEATURES

House & Home has a seasonal quality to it, making it the first place to look if you want to dazzle your family with the perfect Easter buffet, or astound yourself by making your own Christmas cookies this year.

Tools/Guides contains practical home-decorating advice such as the Kitchen Planning Guide, which gives a wealth of useful tips whether your kitchen is a tiny galley or a spacious 'heart-of-the-home' type of place. Use their Interactive Kitchen Arranger, which opens in a separate window, to plan your space using a click-and-drag facility to move appliances and units around. Download Real Player to view videos on creating Faux Finishes. Articles include Quick & Easy, which has simple revamp projects for the home. If you fear you're a social klutz, Table Top Style will save you from yourself, with advice on formal and relaxed table settings – and no, the latter does not involve a sofa and a pizza box the size of a car tyre.

More Guides and Tools is a practical section which includes links to the comprehensive Home Improvement Encyclopaedia.

OTHER FEATURES

For a quick decorating fix, check out Today's Highlights, which includes Your Style and Weekend Fun, for simple projects to add a little zip to your scheme. Crafts contains a good selection of projects if you want to try your hand at knitting, quilting or cross stitch. You can also register to download free projects and patterns. The Discussion Groups are lively, quick to view and generally helpful.

An inspirational site which allows you to move around so easily between sections you hardly have time for your enthusiasm to cool.

www.brightbeige.co.uk
brightbeige

Overall rating: ★ ★ ★ ★ ★		
Classification: Ezine	**Readability:**	★ ★ ★ ★ ★
Updating: Monthly	**Content:**	★ ★ ★ ★ ★
Navigation: ★ ★ ★	**Speed:**	★ ★ ★

UK

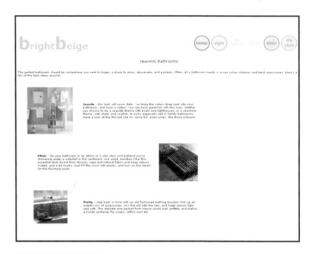

Among the many sites which concentrate on classic, 'grown-up' decorating, Brightbeige is a breath of fresh air, injecting some much-needed fun into home fashion. The brainchild of Trudie Bamford, it provides advice, ideas, and practical help to the aspirational decorator. Essentially young and urban in concept, it is a well-constructed site with links to some of the best online home accessory catalogues. Click on the disc-shaped logos on the right-hand side to navigate between sections.

SPECIAL FEATURES

Style leads you through their archives of refreshing and useful features. Become a Lounge Lizard offers a choice of colour schemes or styles to create the perfect lair. Accessories open up in pop-up windows with links to online catalogues. Make a Rented House Homely gives ideas for this most tricky of decorating problems. Browse through House Basics for tips on Colour, Texture, Light, Your Style, and Your Home.

BB House offers two choices, whether you're planning a room from scratch, or looking for funky shortcuts. Select a room from the drop-down menu. The From Scratch menu has links to their Room Kits.

OTHER FEATURES

Each week, Trudie Bamford and her team select the best online questions and give detailed answers to them. There is also an archive of previous questions, including 'How Can I fit all of my stuff into my tiny bedroom?' and 'What if me and my partner's tastes are opposite?' Shop has an I Want To Shop For ... drop-down menu to allow you to rummage through their excellent, if slightly limited, links. You can also sign up for a free monthly Newsletter.

Brightbeige is one of the few British decorating ezines and deserves much praise for seizing the opportunity this new medium offers. Bookmark it!

www.countryliving.women.com
Country Living

Overall rating: ★ ★ ★ ★ ★			
Classification:	Ezine	Readability:	★ ★ ★ ★ ★
Updating:	Weekly	Content:	★ ★ ★ ★ ★
Navigation:	★ ★ ★ ★	Speed:	★ ★ ★ ★

US

As country as a damp labrador, this site has daily tips, hints on collecting, accessible decorating advice, and information on stylish, informal entertaining. Check out this month's features on the homepage or use the menu bar at the top of the screen to view each section. One of the most appealing things about this site is that, though appearing to be quite smart, much of the advice focuses on affordable transformations and home ideas.

SPECIAL FEATURES

Decorating is a multi-faceted decorators' delight. Room of the Week includes an inspirational photograph. The term 'room' is loosely defined to include garden spaces too. There are practical tips on achieving the look yourself. Clicking on Previous takes you on a tour of other featured rooms. House Tour contains an index of articles on delightful homes with a thumbnail to tempt you to explore further. The houses are predominantly American, although some European ones are featured too. Set your watch before you start the tour; you could lose yourself in this section. Use the drop-down menu to tour their Gallery of Homes by room if you are looking for inspiration for a specific space. If you're feeling retro, House of the Year highlights newly-built houses with a traditional feel. Install the Quicktime plug-in to view some of the houses room by room on a virtual tour. If you want to bring a little bit of The Waltons to your mountain, you can also buy the plans of

these award-winning homes. In Ask the Expert, senior editors on the magazine answer readers' queries.

Entertaining provides seasonal tips on menus and table decorations, and is illustrated with beautiful photographs. You can also access the extensive recipe archive.

OTHER FEATURES

Collecting offers information on antiques, and although it is American, much of the advice on collecting trends is equally applicable in the UK. If you are planning a trip to the USA, check out their state-by-state listing of the best flea markets, craft fairs, and antique shows. For the green-fingered, or -thumbed as the Americans would put it, the Gardening section is an inspiration. If you think that barrowfuls of gravel and a few spiky yucca plants do not a garden make, you will find plenty of ideas here. With lovely photographs of luscious and abundant gardens, Country Living's gardening aesthetic seems to have much in common with traditional English style.

An exemplary site which marries beautiful photographs with practical, clearly expressed information.

www.marthastewart.com
Martha Stewart Online

Overall rating: ★ ★ ★ ★ ★

Classification:	Ezine	Readability:	★ ★ ★ ★ ★
Updating:	Monthly	Content:	★ ★ ★ ★ ★
Navigation:	★ ★ ★ ★	Speed:	★ ★ ★

US 🔒

Enter the world of Martha, where no raffia is left un-plaited, no cookie un-iced. If you thought that life was too short to stress over the symmetrical beauty of your woodpile, the ravishing photographs on this site might just make you think again. It's tied to her US television show, and there are links everywhere to pages of purchasable merchandise, but there are still plenty of practical projects to make a visit to this site worthwhile. Every section contains links to relevant bulletin boards and information on live internet chats with Martha staffers and even with the great decorating goddess herself. In some cases, templates, patterns, and detailed project instructions are presented in portable document format (PDF), which you need Adobe Acrobat to read. You can download this free from the site.

There are many spoof sites parodying the Martha style, but even if her extraordinary attention to detail isn't quite your thing, you'll still be better off visiting this site. For sheer funniness, few of them can match Martha's Rolling Pin Display Case ...

SPECIAL FEATURES

Home displays highlights from the magazine and is updated monthly. Click on the main feature and it will bring you to a page where you can search the archives using More Home Features. These include pieces on Easy Decorating Projects, Collecting Glass & Pottery, and Good Things, a very popular part of the magazine which teaches you how to do everything beautifully, from cleaning mussels, to rustling up your own twig coasters.

Keeping is the place to go if you're still not sure how to make your bed, clean up after yourself or do the laundry. It's all presented with the utmost seriousness, right down to the illustrated, seven-point guide to folding a sweater.

Cooking Look here for seasonal recipes, the suggested menu for the week which appears on the right-hand side of the page, and the interactive Recipe Finder. This works by typing in a keyword and then ticking on boxes to further refine the search. Apple pie brought up a satisfying nine recipes.

OTHER FEATURES

Gardening contains outdoor tasks for the month, arranging flowers, and also a very useful Encyclopaedia of Plants which you can search by soil type or situation to locate exactly the right plant for your plot. Although most of us would baulk at the hefty shipping costs, the Shopping section is still worth looking at if only for the sheer diversity of the products. How do we get through life without crustacean bottle openers, maple leaf pancake moulds, turkey-shaped toothpick holders, and a special little gizmo which looks like a tea strainer and is intended for toasting sesame seeds?

An immaculately designed site which is full of information but looks very streamlined. It's useful for practical advice and for decorating inspiration, so long as you keep your sense of humour. Now go and plait your lawn ...

www.suite101.com

Suite101.com

Overall rating: ★ ★ ★ ★ ★			
Classification:	Information	**Readability:**	★ ★ ★ ★ ★
Updating:	Constantly	**Content:**	★ ★ ★ ★ ★
Navigation:	★ ★ ★ ★	**Speed:**	★ ★ ★

US

Suite101.com is a fabulously practical site dedicated to offering sound advice on almost any topic you can think of. This site is not technically an ezine, but once you're inside it you can browse the magazine-style features for hours. It is divided into Crafts, Collecting, Gardening, Food & Drink, and Home sections, each one containing regularly updated features and relevant links to other helpful sites. For our purposes, all of the pages listed below are to be found in the Home section.

A very busy site which manages to convey masses of information without being overwhelming. One of the best collection of links on the net.

SPECIAL FEATURES

Apartment Living gives advice to this often-forgotten home owner on how to 'turn your unit into a home'. Apartment Life offers many links to useful sites, including www.windowbox.com for the small-scale gardener.

Home Management offers encouragement for the domestically-challenged on juggling bills, cleaning, and home maintenance.

Party Planning If the idea of catering for anything more demanding than a hungry puppy fills you with dread, seek solace in this section with its extensive advice on creating a beautiful table, themed parties, seasonal entertaining, and birthday celebrations. The recipe links are extensive.

Being Thrifty almost sounds like fun, with advice on everything from parsimonious pet ownership to cheapskate weddings.

www.sampler.com/decideas/decideas.html
Country Sampler Decorating Ideas Magazine

Overall rating: ★ ★ ★			
Classification:	Ezine	Readability:	★ ★ ★ ★
Updating:	Monthly	Content:	★ ★ ★ ★
Navigation:	★ ★ ★ ★ ★	Speed:	★ ★ ★
US			

This site is to country decorating what Shania Twain is to country music; a fresh, contemporary, and occasionally gutsy reinterpretation of a traditional style. Bypass Country Sampler Decorating Ideas' site if you're after ruffles and bows, because the style is much cleaner and more pared-down than that. In fact, the look is surprisingly smart. Use the menu down the left-hand side of the page to view the regularly-updated sections.

SPECIAL FEATURES

Projects includes a helpful Archive of features. Instructions are clear and illustrated with detailed photographs which make even the most complicated projects seem achievable. Look out for simple shelving ideas, a lampshade made out a galvanised metal bucket, and something called a Camp Cushion, which is a rustic pillow made form a lattice of fabric scraps rather than something that might appear on Lily Savage's Christmas list.

Technique includes a wide range of stylish projects, from Colourwashing Walls, to the more original Painted Room Dividers, French Farmhouse Walls, and Decoupage Tiles.

Christy's Tips are formulated by Christy Grafton, the magazine's senior designer. Check out this month's ideas and the archives for plenty of New Country inspiration. Before you get too excited, bringing Old World allure to your bedroom has nothing to do with Sean Connery and everything to do with making your retreat cosy for winter.

OTHER FEATURES

Idea Exchange is a message board full of decorating tips and ideas for fresh-air types. Join the realms of Betsys, LuAnnes, and Kristys to exchange problems and solutions in a friendly, chatty list.

If you live in the middle of the city or the heart of the country, this site has a wealth of easily-accessible information on modern rustic decorating.

www.housebeautiful.women.com

House Beautiful

Overall rating: ★ ★ ★ ★			
Classification:	Ezine	Readability:	★ ★ ★ ★ ★
Updating:	Monthly	Content:	★ ★ ★ ★ ★
Navigation:	★ ★ ★	Speed:	★ ★ ★

US

This site combines practical features with lively interactive quizzes and frequently-updated quick tips, making it a pleasant enough place to spend a spare 20 minutes. You can view excerpts from articles in the magazine's current and past issues, but you never get the impression that the site is just an opportunity to rehash old ideas. View the magazine's various sections at the top right-hand side of the page and check out current features on the lower half of the homepage. The Search box at the top of the page is swift and accurate. Wherever you are in the site, you can use the menu along the bottom of the page to move around efficiently.

SPECIAL FEATURES

Decorating introduces readers to Elements of Style, and includes Inspiration of the Week and an archive, which opens in a pop-up window.

Design/Architecture includes regularly updated features on all the latest trends.

Ask Peggy Each week, House Beautiful editor Peggy Kennedy gives a thoughtful answer to a reader's question. Click on Search Peggy's Column By Topic, or type in a keyword to locate the answer to a specific problem. This is a very good resource, with extensive links to related subjects.

OTHER FEATURES

Send your email address to subscribe to the Free Newsletter. Look for message boards under Your Own Home. Helpfully, boards are divided into Making a House Your Home to exchange queries and advice, Renovating for remodelling advice, and special boards for Kitchens and Bathrooms.

A useful and lively site with plenty of design help and decorating inspiration.

www.wallpaper.com
Wallpaper*

Overall rating: ★ ★ ★ ★

Classification:	Ezine	Readability:	★ ★ ★ ★ ★
Updating:	Monthly	Content:	★ ★ ★ ★
Navigation:	★ ★ ★	Speed:	★ ★ ★ ★

UK

This uber-urban style magazine deserves a lot of kudos for its ambitious and sophisticated website which was launched in April 2000. It has used the opportunities that the internet offers to create an innovative, stylish taster of their paper version, and if it's not the 'unforgettable journey' that the introduction voice-over promises, then it is at least an interesting one. The homepage offers a tempting introduction to the features in this month's issue in a pop-up window. Run the cursor over the grid on the lower left and the contents of each section appear. From elsewhere in the site, click on the arrow on the lower right of the page to return to the grid menu. Navigation takes a little while to get used to, but once you do, this site provides a wonderful overview of all things modern.

SPECIAL FEATURES

002Space Click on Wallpaper House at the bottom of the page to view a building conceived by the magazine's editorial director, Tyler Brulé, and architect Thomas Sandall. Click on the plans and then on different areas of the floorplan to view different areas of the house.

003Entertaining Dish of the Week provides smart, easy recipes to fuel your journey through the urban jungle. Our Sommelier Says gives advice on wine. Group Dynamics is an entertaining way to spend a few minutes. Their dinner party seating planner allows you to select a table and then

drag and drop anything up to 16 chairs around it. Seat your guests and put their initials on each chair before printing it out.

009Archive If you've missed an issue or simply want to browse, click on your chosen month and the sections will appear in a strip at the bottom of the page. In theory, you can now click to enter, but on the occasions we tried this, the site seemed to be having teething troubles. This was frustrating as the site leaves you longing for more.

OTHER FEATURES

Go to 001 Intelligence and click on W* Dispatch to register to receive regular updates on the online and paper publication. If the website has whetted your appetite for more, go to 008 W*? to order back issues, get to know the contributors, and find out about subscription details.

A sophisticated site which injects some much-needed wit into the world of design journalism. It is hoped that some of the site's teething troubles are quickly ironed out to make this an even more enjoyable snapshot into the world of peerless chic.

www.christmasorganizing.com/newsinfo.html

ChristmasOrganizing.com

Overall rating: ★ ★ ★

Classification:	Newsletter	Readability:	★ ★ ★
Updating:	Weekly	Content:	★ ★ ★ ★
Navigation:	★ ★ ★	Speed:	★ ★ ★

US R

If all you want for Christmas is a little peace and quiet, then you can't start planning too soon – at least that is the message of this perky American newsletter. So, if you want to spend Christmas day doing nothing more strenuous than singing along to The Wizard of Oz, let this site help you to take the strain out of the festive season.

SPECIAL FEATURES

Holiday Plan Of Action gives advice on creating your own planning notebook to help you organise yourself into a state of festive bliss.

Christmas Preparations gives links to all areas of the site, including creating Gift Boxes to store the gifts you're efficiently squirreling away all year. Holiday Baking includes cookies and other home-made gifts. Holiday Cleaning will ensure that you're not vacuuming the hallway as your guests walk through it. Entertaining gives advice on spreading the load of responsibility in the run-up to Christmas.

A simple site which aims to help you face Christmas with joy in your heart and money in your pocket.

www.homedecoratingsite.com

HomeDecoratingSite.com

Overall rating: ★ ★ ★

Classification:	Ezine	Readability:	★ ★ ★ ★ ★
Updating:	Monthly	Content:	★ ★ ★
Navigation:	★ ★ ★ ★ ★	Speed:	★ ★ ★ ★

US

This site has the feel of a watered-down, highly achievable Martha Stewart. Easy-to-follow decorating and entertaining advice is teamed with regularly-updated tips, making the Martha-lite site appealingly lively. Use the menu bar at the top of the page to move around the site.

SPECIAL FEATURES

Tips by Room is comprehensive in its breadth. Browse here for advice on everything from taking care of household linens, to beginning an art collection, and using mirrors creatively.

Cool Products covers reviews of household equipment. Some of these are only available in America, but reviews are accompanied by more general advice. For example, a piece on a coffee maker expands to include general advice on brewing a great cup of java.

Hot Trends features one aspect of contemporary home care each month, with further room-by-room advice and ideas located down the right-hand side of the page.

A promising, well-laid-out site. which provides enthusiastic and accessible household advice. We hope it continues to improve, and that depth will come to match presentation.

www.livingandentertaining.com
Living

Overall rating: ★ ★ ★			
Classification:	Newsletter	**Readability:**	★ ★ ★ ★
Updating:	Monthly	**Content:**	★ ★ ★ ★
Navigation:	★ ★ ★ ★	**Speed:**	★ ★ ★

US

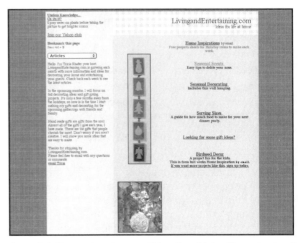

A straightforward and accessible site which offers plenty of easy projects for decorating on a shoestring.

This is a homey, practical newsletter edited by Tricia Shafer, who claims she was born creative, as her mother seized the opportunity of a protracted labour to finish off a cushion cover. She trained in fashion design, and on moving to Manhattan, high rents forced her to transfer her design skills to creating inexpensive and stylish decorating ideas. Use the drop-down box to search through articles or peruse the seasonal projects on the homepage.

SPECIAL FEATURES

Articles Choose Decorating from the drop-down menu for archived features, displayed with thumbnails, listed by month. Generally, the emphasis is on small projects which home owners can carry out using things they already have around the house, or with supplies that can be bought cheaply from most hardware shops. There are plenty of ideas for instant decorative pick-me-ups such as changing furniture placement, picture hanging, or using plants and flowers. Seasonal Decorating includes easy step-by-steps for making pomanders, pumpkin candles, and wreathes. Home Inspirations gives details of small, finishing-touch projects such as decoupage, making napkin rings, and rag rugs.

OTHER FEATURES

Sign up to receive a free newsletter containing decorative tips and ideas.

OTHER SITES OF INTEREST

Beme.com
www.beme.com

This general-interest site aimed at young women is visually arresting, if a little labour-intensive. For home-interest features, go to Section Three, Home Life, and then click on Nest. The emphasis is on lifestyle rather than practical decorating pieces, which is rather a disappointment, as the site is brought to us by ipc, one of the country's biggest magazine publishers with many decorating titles in its stable. It's a shame that they don't see this site as an opportunity to allow web users access to their extensive archive of features. All in all, what there is in this site is rather good, but the glossy design raises expectations which the rather thin content fails to satisfy.

Country Life
www.countrylife.co.uk

This quintessentially traditional magazine is to be congratulated on venturing onto the internet when many of its more contemporary rivals have failed to do so. Use the drop-down menu to search among Antiques, Architecture, and Fine Art, or simply browse through the breathtaking houses in Property News. Use the Regional Guide to find local antique dealers and fairs. Country Shop gives good online shopping links to suitably tony retailers; make this your first stop for hampers and cigars.

HomeArts
www.homearts.com

General interest American ezine covering family, beauty, and home. Use the menu on the right to navigate. There are daily 'specials', with Thursday being Home & Garden day. Clicking on Home takes you to the Shelter section with The Handyman's column on home maintenance and decorating. Go to Inside Shelter for a digest of features and columns from American House Beautiful, Country Living, Good Housekeeping, and Victoria magazines.

Ladies' Home Journal Online
www.lhj.com

This is the site of the popular American women's magazine. For the decorator, its main attraction is the interactive Furniture Arranger listed under Special Features which allows you to try out different floor plans. Go to Getting Started on the right-hand side of the page and click on What You Will Need To Load Free Shockwave 8 Plug-In; it takes about 10 to 12 minutes to load. Select the room layout you want to play with from Bedroom, Home Office, or Living Room, and then feed in your room dimensions. Now the fun starts – select architectural details such as windows, fireplaces, and doors to replicate your room. Then, as you arrange furniture by clicking and dragging from the drop-down menu, relevant decorating tips appear in a box on the right.

STYLE-revolution
www.style-revolution.com

This lively ezine is the creation of HomePro.com (see also p. 20), and is full of ideas on the latest home trends and decorative techniques. There are lots of competitions, giveaways, and links, and features are regularly updated, so there's always something new to look at. Use the menu along the top of the page to move between sections; run the cursor along the list and the title of this month's feature will appear on the screen. Graham's Advice is a makeover project devised by interior designer Graham Wynn. The text on achieving the look yourself is rather dense and small, but it's worth persevering with for the clear advice it contains. All of the products used are listed with prices and stockists' phone numbers.

Chapter 5

antiques and architectural salvage

When Caroline Aherne's Royle Family sit around betting on the Antiques Roadshow's appraisers' valuations, you know that the passion for antiques has spread right across the British social spectrum. Surprisingly, the world's newest way of communicating lends itself well to one of its most traditional spheres, that of the antique and architectural salvage trades. As well as providing instant access to dealers' stock and auction houses' lots, many of the best sites have fascinating features on price trends, specialist collecting and care and restoration.

Few of the sites allow you to buy directly online. That part of the transaction is usually carried out the old fashioned way, by telephone, but it must be the simplest way of searching for a special object. This is particularly true of the architectural salvage sites. A few minutes on the web can replace wearisome weekends driving from scruffy yard to overwhelming warehouse in search of the perfect reclaimed radiator or bathtub. If you're the kind of person who can't walk past a skip without looking inside, replace skip surfing with web surfing. At least you can do it from the comfort of your own home.

www.antiques.co.uk
antiques.co.uk

Overall rating: ★ ★ ★ ★ ★			
Classification:	Ecommerce	Readability:	★ ★ ★ ★ ★
Updating:	Weekly	Content:	★ ★ ★ ★ ★
Navigation:	★ ★ ★ ★	Speed:	★ ★ ★ ★

UK

This new site, founded in May 2000, is art and antiques for the dotcom generation. The brainchild of an art historian, lawyer, antique dealer, city banker, and web expert, it is an almost perfect blend of their individual talents. If you want to begin or add to your own collection, or simply want to learn more about the fine and decorative arts, antiques.co.uk holds a wealth of information.

The site is edited by Dr Freddie Law-Turner, who trained at the Courtauld Institute, and she brings academic rigour as well as her good eye for design to this clear and elegant site. The wide range of stock, from whimsical pieces of porcelain to entire suites of what the dealers call 'important furniture', is clearly photographed and it is easy to move around between sections without losing yourself in a labyrinth of tulip wood and lapis lazuli. The simple yet chic design of the site means that though the stock is extensive, searching for individual pieces is swift.

SPECIAL FEATURES

Showroom lists current stock by category, from arms and armour, to toys. When you select an item it is displayed with its price, and if that piques your interest, you can view more details and save the piece to your portfolio. Unlike many antique sites, you can buy online by credit or debit card via a secure site.

If you are particularly keen on an object, antiques.co.uk will arrange a viewing with the seller in return for a deposit, refundable if you decide not to buy.

Reviews and Events This section provides a comprehensive guide to exhibitions and antiques fairs across the country and abroad. An ever-increasing archive of features by the country's leading authorities gives a great introduction to collecting and price trends. Established experts such as Godfrey Barker, who has written on the art market for the Daily Telegraph, The Times and The Evening Standard, and Hugo Morley-Fletcher, former head of Christie's European Ceramics and Glass Department, share their knowledge and expertise in a clear and accessible manner, so if you're an arts afficionado or a mere beginner, there's plenty in this elegant, informative site for you.

Guarantee Antiques.co.uk are so proud of their Safety Code that they claim it's safer to buy through them than on the High Street or at auction. Every piece is vetted online by an expert and guaranteed for condition and authenticity by a Lloyd's of London underwriter to protect the buyer from deliberate fraud by the seller. Also, if you find that Biedermeier chair just isn't right with your Louis XIV bureau, you can return it up to seven working days after delivery and receive a full refund. In some circumstances they may even pay for the return shipping and, in any event, their insurance will cover the piece while in transit.

OTHER FEATURES

If you're looking for a particular item, the Advanced Search facility allows you to quick-search the whole site. If the search still doesn't turn up what you're looking for, it automatically goes to an email page where customers are able to leave a description of the piece they're after, its approximate dimensions, and a suggested price range.

When the experts are not appearing on the Antiques Roadshow, they're writing for this site.

www.finelot.com
Finelot

Overall rating: ★ ★ ★ ★ ★			
Classification: Company		**Readability:**	★ ★ ★ ★ ★
Updating: Weekly		**Content:**	★ ★ ★ ★ ★
Navigation: ★ ★ ★ ★		**Speed:**	★ ★ ★ ★

(UK)

Finelot, the art, antiques and luxury goods group, was created in 1999 with BBC Antiques Roadshow expert and fourth-generation antique dealer John Bly at the helm. This is an appropriate place for him to be as he is a distant relation of Captain Bly of Mutiny on the Bounty fame. This seems to be a happy ship, however, and its website is injected with sufficient amounts of Bly's good humour to prevent it from being stuffy and intimidating. Over 160 antique dealers trade through this site, and more than 10,000 items are on display with a total worth of more than £40m. My only criticism, and it is a small one, is that some of the photographs could be more extensively captioned.

SPECIAL FEATURES

Bly's Bounty is a regularly updated section which reflects the personal preoccupations and detailed knowledge of the site's founder. Take a look at Bly's Weekly Insight, a lucid and informative essay on types of furniture such as tallboy chests and sofa tables. He gets the balance right between the history of furniture and current pricing news.

Forum This section aims to provide a place where collectors, dealers, and customers can ask for advice and 'talk shop'; however, the number of discussion threads seems limited, perhaps due to the relative newness of the site. Even glib questions are treated to a thoughtful and prompt response from Mr Bly though. For example, when one questioner asks if there is a relationship between Chippendale furniture and Chippendale dancers, Mr Bly replies in the affirmative, saying that both have cabriole legs, attractive ankles, and tiny drawers.

OTHER FEATURES

Highstyle is perfect for a little fantasy browsing. If you already have an antique collection to rival the Queen's, check in here to browse through some prime horseflesh, pick out a dream holiday or even bid on a financial forecast from one of the world's leading astrologers. Her first line should be 'you've just found yourself at least $1,500 lighter,' as that, indeed, is where bids start ... A superstitious lot, the filthy rich.

Although at first glance this site looks a little too jet-set to be of any practical use to most of us, it is exemplary in its accessibility and goes a long way towards demistifying the smartest end of a very smart trade. And when John Bly says Finelot can track down everything from a Picasso, to a palomino pony, you're inclined to believe him.

www.qxl.com/hugh/w/of/antiques
Hugh Scully's World of Antiques

Overall rating: ★ ★ ★ ★ ★			
Classification: Valuation		**Readability:**	★ ★ ★ ★ ★
Updating: Varies		**Content:**	★ ★ ★ ★ ★
Navigation: ★ ★ ★ ★		**Speed:**	★ ★ ★

UK

Hugh Scully has thrown in his Antiques Roadshow map and taken up with web auctioneers qxl to produce this very useful site dedicated to valuing, and possibly selling, antiques and collectibles. It is approachable and friendly, reflecting today's widespread interest in antiques and collecting. Like many qxl pages, however, it can be slow to navigate, as it is so graphically intensive.

SPECIAL FEATURES

Valuations are the central feature of this site. Use the very straightforward tour to familiarise yourself with the site's valuation and auction facility. Fill out a detailed form about your piece, attach an image, and pay five pounds to receive an expert's appraisal in four working days, which you access using a personal qxl password. If you decide to auction your piece, it will be displayed with a special World of Antiques icon, which allows interested buyers to read the expert's verdict before placing a bid.

Meet the Experts gives biographies of the site's valuers, a gaggle of media-savvy auctioneers, dealers, and writers on antiques and collectibles, many of whom have appeared on the Antiques Roadshow, The Great Antiques Hunt, and Collector's Lot.

Collectors' Club provides Beginners' Guides to collecting a wide range of things, from silver and porcelain to pottery and furniture. The Masterclass Guides give more detail but are more limited in number. They are welcome, however, because many of the most popular sites are great for beginners but have little to interest the more experienced and knowledgeable collector.

OTHER FEATURES

Daily News from the world of art and antiques is worth perusing, whether your interest is in Tracey Emin's bed, or limited edition statuettes of the Queen Mother.

What's On provides a comprehensive guide to exhibitions, fairs and auctions.

A refreshing, if slightly slow, site which will appeal to those intimidated by the rarified world of the traditional auction houses.

www.lapada.co.uk
LAPADA

Overall rating: ★ ★ ★ ★ ★			
Classification:	Society	**Readability:**	★ ★ ★ ★ ★
Updating:	Varies	**Content:**	★ ★ ★ ★ ★
Navigation:	★ ★ ★ ★	**Speed:**	★ ★ ★ ★

UK

If you're wary about buying antiques because you think the dealers have the ethics of Del Boy and the pricing policy of Lovejoy, this is the site that will allow you to rest peacefully in your Nineteenth Century walnut lit en bâteau. Whether you're interested in Roman coins or contemporary fine art, LAPADA is the largest association of professional dealers in the country, with over 700 members. This smart-looking site inspires confidence. Click on Index and Overview for a summary of all that the site offers, including a guide to the association's code of practice. Many of the members listed are private dealers who work on an appointment-only basis, so this site gives you access to professionals you wouldn't necessarily find by wandering down the High Street.

SPECIAL FEATURES

Directory of Members helps you to find dealers by region and then by county by clicking on a map directory. There are links to dealers' own websites if they have them and details of specialist shippers and handlers to allow you to get your booty home safely.

Care and Security of Antiques suggests how to preserve your cherished pieces. If you've ever wondered how to make your own silver polishing cloths or puzzled over how best to store that ugly but valuable family portrait, you'll find the answers here. There are also helpful links to specialist restoration services if DIY seems like a DI-DON'T.

Buying and Selling Antiques is a succinct and accessible guide for the tyro collector. It also includes a comprehensive guide to antique shops around the country, with addresses of their members and links where they have them. This section includes a great piece on Buying Antiques in London, informative for natives and visitors alike. Click on a map of London to select an area, and further refine your search by postcode. The directory gives a brief description of each area, its best streets for antique fiends, and lists its local registered dealers. It also gives the nearest Underground station and some other helpful titbits of information for out-of-towners, for example, stating that Alfie's Antique Market is close to Lords Cricket Ground.

OTHER FEATURES

You can register to receive press releases, their online magazine, and other LAPADA news by email. There are also good links to up-to-date price indexes, insurers, and the Due Diligence Directory of police contacts. The facility for searching for individual items is at an early stage. They can point you in the direction of a dealer who may be able to help, but offer nothing more specific than that. Given the high standard of the rest of the site, however, it can't be too long before this facility catches up with the rest.

A well-designed and interesting site which provides a clear and authoritative guide to the antiques trade.

www.arcsal.com
Arcsal Architectural Antiques

Overall rating: ★ ★ ★ ★			
Classification:	Business	Readability:	★ ★ ★ ★ ★
Updating:	Continuously	Content:	★ ★ ★ ★ ★
Navigation:	★ ★ ★ ★	Speed:	★ ★ ★

UK

Whether you're seeking 1,000 Edwardian bricks, a cast-iron bath or a seventeenth-century oak front door, this treasure trove of reclaimed materials should be your first port of call. The idea for this site came to David Willis, one of Arcsal's directors, after he spent ten years restoring his seventeenth-century stone farmhouse and realised he could have saved himself many precious weekends in the car if this resource had been available to him online.

The catalogue of stock is easily and swiftly accessible by clicking on the appropriate thumbnail for each section. Every item is illustrated with a good, clear photograph, a simple description, a note on condition, and its dimensions in inches. Prices don't include delivery or VAT; these are negotiated with Arcsal depending on your location. They hold many items at their base in Castle Cary, Somerset. For other pieces, they act as a broker between buyer and seller.

SPECIAL FEATURES

Catalogue of Stock is divided into Bath and Kitchen, Church Architecture, Doors and Gates, Furniture, Gardens, Lighting, Radiators and Fireplaces, and Reclaimed Materials, all illustrated by thumbnails. Perhaps the most intriguing category for the casual browser is the section entitled Whimsies where, at the time of writing, stock included a traditional red and white barber's pole and a Russian T34 army tank. If only one had the room ...

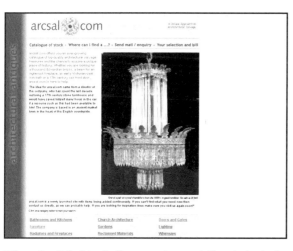

arcsal com offers you an ever-growing catalogue of top-quality architectural salvage treasures and the chance to acquire a unique piece of history. Whether you are looking for a thousand Edwardian bricks, a beam for an inglenook fireplace, or early Victorian cast iron bath or a 17th century oak front door, arcsal.com is here to help.

The idea for arcsal.com came from a director of the company, who has spent the last decade restoring a 17th century stone farmhouse and would have saved himself many hours in the car if a resource such as this had been available to him! The company is based in an ancient market town in the heart of the English countryside.

One of a pair of crystal chandeliers from the 1900's in good condition. On sale at £1,540

arcsal.com is a newly launched site with items being added continuously. If you can't find what you need now then contact us directly, as we can probably help. If you are looking for inspiration then make sure you visit us again soon!

Click on a category below to start your search.

Bathrooms and Kitchens	Church Architecture	Doors and Gates
Furniture	Gardens	Lighting
Radiators and Fireplaces	Reclaimed Materials	Whimsies

Where Can I Find A ...? allows you to search the whole site by keyword. If you can't find exactly what you want on their site, you can contact them directly with a description of the item you're seeking and they'll do their best to find it for you.

A well-thought-out site worth visiting for the sheer variety of its stock.

www.bafra.org.uk
British Antique Furniture Restorers' Association

Overall rating: ★ ★ ★ ★			
Classification: Society		**Readability:**	★ ★ ★ ★
Updating: Monthly		**Content:**	★ ★ ★ ★ ★
Navigation: ★ ★ ★		**Speed:**	★ ★ ★ ★

UK

In these days when you can scarcely turn on the television without seeing some gimlet-eyed punter waiting breathlessly as an expert appraises granny's old whatnot, there are few of us who do not know that shoddy restoration of an old piece of furniture can ruin its value forever. In the war against the weekend warrior, armed with his crevice tool and tin of stripper, BAFRA is the first line of defence. It is a national organisation of craftsmen and women who specialise in the delicate field of antique restoration and conservation. Entry into BAFRA is suitably difficult and exclusive. Members have to have five years of full-time experience in the profession and show a high level of achievement in cabinetmaking and finishing skills, as well as a comparable level of expertise in at least one other field, such as gilding or lacquerwork. They also need to demonstrate a thorough knowledge of furniture history. Given that attention to detail is a prerequisite for entry into this exclusive band, it is rather a shame that their site is more practical than beautiful. Persevere through the rather dry and old-fashioned presentation however, and there is much to be gleaned from this site.

SPECIAL FEATURES

Finding a Conservator-Restorer Search through over 100 full members to find one in your area. Not all counties are covered, but there is a good spread from North Yorkshire to Devon, as well as members in Scotland, Wales, and

Northern Ireland. There are links to members' sites when they have them, though a brief description of members' areas of expertise would be useful too.

Articles are written mainly for the experts, and written by experts rather than by writers, so they don't necessarily leap from the page propelled only by the vividness of their prose. However, there is still plenty to interest the amateur owner or collector. Look out for tips on combating the terrors of central heating (hide your humidifier behind a pot plant) and good, practical advice on the care of antiques from John WL Kitchen, MBE, former head of conservation at the Victoria & Albert Museum.

OTHER FEATURES

BAFRA News gives details of courses and demonstrations, many of which are open to non-members. Tours of stately homes and collections are lead by experts and often give access to pieces not generally on view to the general public. There's a good selection of links to other sites, such as English Heritage, The National Trust, and many museum sites.

If you have anything in your home older than you are, check out this site. What it lacks in pizzazz it more than makes up for in content. Be prepared to scroll, though.

www.bbc.co.uk/antiques
BBC Online Antiques on the Web

Overall rating: ★ ★ ★ ★			
Classification:	TV homepage	**Readability:**	★ ★ ★ ★
Updating:	Weekly	**Content:**	★ ★ ★ ★ ★
Navigation:	★ ★ ★	**Speed:**	★ ★ ★

UK

A large and informative site, multifaceted and well illustrated as we might expect from the BBC. The information is clearly written and easily accessible for those with a burgeoning or casual interest in antiques; there is perhaps a little less of interest to the more advanced connoisseur. Work from the pull-down menu at the top of the homepage to navigate quickly between the many sections.

SPECIAL FEATURES

Features includes concise and informed advice for owners and collectors. If you're entrepreneurially minded, check out the feature on investment buying which includes ceramics expert and Antiques Roadshow veteran David Battie's top tips on building a collection. If you're worried about looking like a beginner on the antiques fair circuit, Terms of the Trade is a must. You'll no longer think that a marriage involves warm champagne and embarrassing relations, or that a sleeper has anything to do with railway tracks or Woody Allen.

Roadshow Finds is perhaps the most interesting of the various sections. Browse through the many categories or try a more specific antique hunt by searching by style, date, the location where the item appeared, or even by the expert who appraised it. For the nosy, there are even details of the owners' stories.

Tricks of the Trade is a fascinating section with simple, straightforward tips on cleaning silver, removing wine stains from rugs, getting rid of water or heat marks on wood, and cleaning stained linen.

OTHER FEATURES

Children's Roadshow is a good idea and a great piece of fun for the pocket money connoisseur. It could be expanded to make it even more appealing.

Quiz is a pleasant enough displacement activity if you're stalled on the crossword and still can't face the washing up.

Antique of the Week highlights a piece of particular interest.

Careers in Antiques is informative if you want to turn your passion into profit.

This site has masses to offer if you're developing an interest in antiques. It's frequently updated, so there's always something new to look at.

www.conservationbuildingproducts.co.uk
Conservation Building Products Limited

Overall rating: ★ ★ ★			
Classification:	Business	Readability:	★ ★ ★
Updating:	Varies	Content:	★ ★ ★
Navigation:	★ ★ ★	Speed:	★ ★ ★ ★

UK

The site of this West Midlands building materials firm could do with some tweaking to make it more useful to the non-trade buyer, but it is an excellent repository for authentic construction supplies. The site looks a little old-fashioned, and its brown, marbled background, difficult-to-read gothic script, and large coat of arms (motto: Built with labour and conserved with love.) just adds to its rather Dungeons-and-Dragons appearance. You can't buy directly from the site, but it gives a good overview of what they hold in their warehouse. Their aim is to provide, from stock, materials suitable for most situations, whether you're extending your home or merely restoring it. Great emphasis is given to their ability to match the age, colour, texture, and degree of weathering on your home's existing structure in order to meet the stringent specifications of town planners.

SPECIAL FEATURES

Gallery of projects and products is accessed by clicking on thumbnails. These include a retro pub built entirely with 90,000 of their bricks, and an old house completely reroofed with their reclaimed tile. Acres of decorative brick, weathered tile, and wooden timbers are displayed, reassuringly, along workmanlike shelving just like you'd find in B&Q.

Products could do with a lot more detail. It is understandably difficult to give specific details about the often unique items traded in architectural salvage, but simply listing examples of the kind of products available is a rather lacklustre way of enticing potential buyers. Some pictures, with guide prices, would enhance the appeal of this site enormously.

Extraordinary Stock promises much but delivers little. In fact, it merely lists some of the more unusual pieces they have stocked, such as cupolas, gazebos, complete panelled rooms, and Victorian summerhouses. Again, some pictures, please.

OTHER FEATURES

At the time of writing, the site's Special Offers page was still under construction. We look forward to prices felled in the reclaimed timber department. Site exits to Yahoo.com.

A promising site which, as yet, is restricted in its usefulness by its old-fashioned design and limited product information.

www.salvo.co.uk
SalvoWEB

Overall rating: ★ ★ ★			
Classification:	Company	Readability:	★ ★
Updating:	Regularly	Content:	★ ★ ★ ★ ★
Navigation:	★ ★ ★	Speed:	★ ★ ★

UK

One of the most established names in the architectural salvage industry, Salvo was set up in 1992 to make it easier to buy and sell old building materials and to create a networking tool for the trade.

More functional than beautiful, their site is overwhelming at first, with 72 links on the opening page. Once you get past that, it contains a wealth of salvage information unrivalled by almost any other site. SalvoWEB is also frequently updated, not just with information on materials, but with other, more newsy, items which may affect people in the trade. For example, at the time of writing it included the latest announcements on the fuel crisis to assist those involved in transporting pieces across the country. This might be the crux of the problem with this site. There's a great deal of imagination and energy put into making it as informative and relevant as possible, but in the haste to get all of this information across, the site's design has rather gone by the wayside. It's jumbled and frustrating to navigate.

In 2001, they intend to introduce video streaming, allowing buyers to visit showrooms and yards online and have a good rummage without needing to update your tetanus.

SPECIAL FEATURES

Dealers provides details of your local showrooms and warehouses. Hundreds of thumbnail photographs allow you to create the most exotic of shopping baskets, whether it's antique elm floorboards you seek, or Tower Hill flagstones, or even a suitably distressed cider press.

Demolition Alerts Though primarily of interest to the building trade, the more adventurous home renovator could find plenty of exciting bargains here. It's an up-to-date list of about-to-be-dismantled properties, from old hospitals and churches, to an entire 10-bedroom Edwardian villa.

Theft Alert lists recently stolen items by description and location. This part of the site seems to be updated daily.

OTHER FEATURES

Since 1990, Salvo has been involved in creating a simple code for dealers in architectural antiques, garden ornaments, and building materials. The huge prices reclaimed items now fetch mean that the shady edges of this industry are beset with vandals who thieve fireplaces from empty houses and rip up paving stones from town centres in the middle of the day. Salvo's voluntary code seeks to encourage a sensible working practice, which involves not dealing in items with a suspect provenance.

There are dozens of links to their advertisers and architectural salvage dealers across the country.

If you're renovating a house, Salvo is a fantastic resource. However, the site would be greatly improved by an overhaul of its design.

OTHER SITES OF INTEREST

Antiques at Antiqnet
www.antiqnet.com
This US site calls itself 'the finest selection of art, antiques, and collectibles on the internet'. Since 1995, they have set up European offices or partnerships in the United Kingdom, France, Italy, Spain, and Germany, but the American bias is still strong. The site is so vast it is difficult to excavate the British sites from the rest, but it's worth persevering, particularly if your interest is in more recent collectibles such as Bakelite or 1950s comics.

Bonhams
www.bonhams.com
A pleasing, quick site with up-to-date information on events and auctions at Bonhams salerooms across the world. There is also information on valuation days, held throughout the United Kingdom, when you can bring in your own pieces to be valued. If you're interested in selling, there are also details on how to arrange for one of their experts to come to your home or bank for an appraisal.

Christie's
www.christies.com
The stylish and simple site of this large auction house manages to balance being authoritative with being user-friendly. Check out the auction calendar for Christie's throughout the world – you can even take a virtual tour of their Paris saleroom if you don't want to run to the expense of the Eurostar. Browse through catalogues for past and current sales, which helpfully and speedily come up in a separate window when you click on their description in the calendar. The Lotfinder facility helps to locate any lot in any Christie's auction in one click. You can even do a little fantasy homes and garden shopping by clicking on the Christie's Great Estates section.

Guinevere Antiques Online
www.guinevere.co.uk

The sumptuous site of Genevieve Weaver's King's Road antique emporium, Guinevere. The store's real charm comes from the combining of eclectic objects imaginatively in stylish room settings, and this has made it a great favourite with interior designers and celebrities such as Anouska Hempel, Jasper Conran, and Elton John. The website manages to recreate something of this flavour, though it is slightly slow to navigate. You can store chosen pieces in a notebook, and then register your interest online. The store will contact you to discuss prices and shipping.

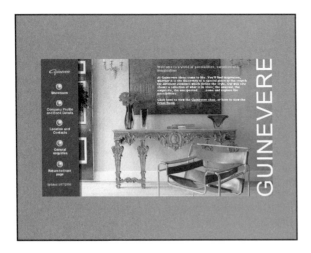

icollector.com
www.icollector.com

This is a full site, but it's very clearly laid out and simple to navigate between the sections. If you're a keen auction-goer or watcher, the catalogue archive contains a breathtaking 600,000 entries dating back to 1994. View by date, location, or category to find estimated values. Although this is an American site, United Kingdom auction houses are very well represented. The site also contains some excellent essays on collecting by English antiques guru, Judith Miller, whose breadth of knowledge is matched by her clarity of expression.

LASSCO
www.lassco.co.uk

LASSCO has been a great favourite with magazine stylists and house renovators for years. If you can't make the pilgrimage to their warehouse, tucked away in an old church on the edge of the City of London, this website is a good place to start. It covers the main features of the LASSCO empire, from garden ornaments through bathroom paraphernalia, radiators, replica architectural elements, and other more esoteric items, such as theatre seats, columns, and chandeliers.

Phillips
www.phillips-auctions.com

Phillips auction house pioneered online evaluation when they developed their own CD-ROM onto which customers can scan their pieces without the bother of trying to cram them into the back of a Range Rover. They also created the computerised Phillips Inventory Management system which allows you to store text and images on a CD-ROM to help you record your collection as well as providing extra peace of mind in the event of loss or theft. Given that they're so computer-savvy, their own site is a little limited in its appeal. The raw-liver background tint to some of the pages such as Phillips News makes the casual viewer disinclined to continue with the search.

Sotheby's
www.sothebys.com

A grand and expansive site covering Sotheby's worldwide operation. Unfortunately, it's rather slow to navigate even in the sparsely illustrated areas and can be difficult to sort the United Kingdom wheat from the rest of the world chaff. An

attempt to find out about education programmes in the United Kingdom proved frustrating and, ultimately, disappointing as it contained only the briefest of details which excluded both cost and the names of the teachers. Sotheby's Connoisseur, their online magazine, is one of the highlights of the site. It is enthusiastically and informatively written by some of the world's leading experts in the fine and decorative arts. Also interesting, was the advice on 'collateralizing your collection'. That's pawn, to you and me...

register now at

www.thegoodwebguide.co.uk

for free updates and new website reviews

housekeeping

The plethora of home advice sites on the internet are predominantly American, and usually none the worse for that. They are a great example of how modern technology conspires to make the world a smaller place, fostering a sense of community with practical, economical, and often traditional remedies to everyday household problems.

These sites are repositories of the kind of wisdom your grandmother might have passed on to you, if she wasn't too busy perfecting her paso doble, or your mother could have suggested if she hadn't been preoccupied with earning a living. Ignore the occasional 'cutesiness', and there is a wealth of information on organising, cleaning, and budgeting.

A final tip: if these sites continue to flourish, it might be worth buying shares in manufacturers of baking soda and vinegar. It seems there's no household ill they cannot cure.

www.allabouthome.com

AllAboutHome.com

Overall rating: ★ ★ ★ ★ ★

Classification:	Advice	**Readability:**	★ ★ ★ ★
Updating:	Frequently	**Content:**	★ ★ ★ ★ ★
Navigation:	★ ★ ★	**Speed:**	★ ★ ★ ★

US

The company ServiceMaster are self-styled 'home care specialists' and, indeed, they are one of the US's largest providers of carpet cleaners, lawn care experts, domestic appliance servicing, and bug fumigation services. Their website is packed with sensible advice and, for a corporate site, it is pleasantly devoid of pushy company propaganda. Some of the advice is specific to American homeowners, but plenty of it is not.

The homepage is clearly laid out and easy to navigate. Seasonal home care features, on subjects such as improving energy efficiency and saving water, are frequently updated. Use the efficient search facility on the top left of the screen, or scroll down the extensive menu along the left-hand side of the screen if you are merely browsing. One word of caution: if you share your home with a cat, turn down the volume on your computer before you go to this site. The tweeting bird noises that accompany the homepage will send your pet into a curtain-climbing feline frenzy.

SPECIAL FEATURES

Home Tips includes Appliance Center, which goes to a menu of different household appliances. Click on one of the appliances for detailed troubleshooting advice on common problems before you start forking out for call-out fees. Comfortingly, ServiceMaster resists the temptation to hawk expensive products and services. For example, if your dishwasher has stopped drying properly, they suggest running a cup of vinegar through the rinse cycle to get rid of mineral deposits on the heating element that may compromise its efficiency. This section also includes a Furniture slot with plenty of useful care tips, such as using mayonnaise to remove water marks on wood and shoe polish to hide small scratches in dark furniture.

Moving is a good section on preparing your home for sale with a helpful week-by-week countdown to moving day.

Safety Sensible advice on Burglary Prevention, Fire Protection, and Kitchen Safety.

Ask the Expert Email ServiceMaster with a specific enquiry, and they endeavour to reply within two working days. When we tried this, a response came back 12 hours later.

OTHER FEATURES

This includes a Virtual Tour of the ServiceMaster house, from attic to basement, outlining common problems home owners might suffer in each area, and their usual solutions. The Message Boards are divided into rooms of the house and are blissfully simple to navigate. Try using their search facility to highlight your specific problem to avoid trawling through masses of messages which aren't pertinent to you. Admittedly, there are far more questions than answers, but what responses there are seem well informed.

An exemplary site for its clarity and breadth. This should be a first stop for anyone with a household problem.

www.organizedhome.com

Organizedhome.com

Overall rating: ★ ★ ★ ★			
Classification:	Ezine	**Readability:**	★ ★ ★ ★
Updating:	Monthly	**Content:**	★ ★ ★ ★ ★
Navigation:	★ ★ ★	**Speed:**	★ ★ ★

US

This site's subtitle is 'organize/declutter/simplify/clean', and it aims to help its readers do just that, without the usual down-home cuteness of many similar sites. In fact, this site is pleasingly clean in its lay-out and stylish in its design. It's edited by Cynthia Townley Ewer, who refers to herself throughout as CEO, for Cynthia Ewer, Organized, and also writes many of the features. Her distinctive brand of good sense and good humour has lead to this site becoming an USA Today Hot Site.

The homepage has lots of links to the site's various sections and many frequently-updated features. Use the pull down bar at the top-right-hand side of the page to explore specific areas of the site or spend an enjoyable few minutes browsing through the many links.

SPECIAL FEATURES

Clean Sweep is a useful little section which includes Cleaning Lessons from the Pros, Magic Minimum: Cleaning Secrets of Busy Families and a Spring Cleaning Chore Checklist. Like the rest of the site, its unstuffy approach makes you think you might even enjoy going at that tile grout with a toothbrush.

Declutter Journal is full of step-by-step advice for those of us who get anxious even contemplating looking inside our wardrobes. There's advice on tackling all of the rooms in the

house. Check out The Clutterer Within: Beating Your Internal Clutter Monster.

Freezer Cooking may be a saviour if you're very busy and tired of living on takeaways. The Get Started Guide explains how, by putting aside a few spare hours, you can cook enough meals for a month and live from your freezer. The Sample Game Plan gives a good idea of how it all works.

Time and Money includes A Tightwad's Guide to Getting Organized, lots of links to free, printable planning pages, and their own Household Notebook.

OTHER FEATURES

Subscribe to their free monthly Newsletter, make a note of their seasonal cleaning Checklists, and browse the Message Boards. There are separate message boards for each section, and all seem busy, with sometimes dozens of responses to queries. Don't be put off by all the smiley faces; advice is often thoughtful and well informed.

One of the few home advice sites that doesn't make you feel like you should be wearing a floral apron while you read it. A refreshingly modern site for those seeking domestic advice or organizational inspiration, it could do with a little tweaking to make navigating between sections simpler.

www.simpleliving101.com/cleaning.html
Simple Living 101

Overall rating: ★ ★ ★ ★			
Classification:	Advice	**Readability:**	★ ★ ★
Updating:	Frequently	**Content:**	★ ★ ★ ★
Navigation:	★ ★ ★ ★	**Speed:**	★ ★ ★ ★

(US)

This cleaning page is part of the award-winning Simple Living 101 website. More friendly than worthy, the site proclaims its aim of 'getting back to basics' in an enthusiastic and inspirational manner, suitably tempered with a strong dose of common sense. Easy recipes for environmentally friendly housekeeping are plentiful, practical and easy to find. Use the menu at the top of the page to explore the site's many features. After all that cleaning, you may wish to peruse the Beauty section and its almost edible recipes for face masks, hand lotions, and hair conditioners.

SPECIAL FEATURES

Kitchen offers quick, inexpensive remedies to common household problems. Check out air fresheners using orange peel and vanilla essence, making your own household cleaners, and advice on tackling troublesome projects like cleaning cast-iron pans. Recipes for cleaning solutions use ingredients you probably have in your kitchen anyway and are simple and environmentally friendly. Most are very good, but the homemade paste for cleaning silver, which uses salt, might be a little too abrasive for more delicate pieces. Endearingly, they ask for advice on things they're stuck on themselves.

Living Room Some tips are repeated from other sections, but the carpet cleaning solutions are good and effective. The baking soda method they suggest is particularly useful for fine carpets and rugs, as it cleans and removes odours without damaging delicate fibres.

Home Organization tips are cheap and easy. Try using vinegar in the rinse cycle instead of fabric softener, and cleaning windows with a spray bottle filled with soda water.

Advice on systematically culling and organizing clutter is inspirational, as are the many money- saving suggestions.

Under Sink Cupboard encourages us to junk the toxic cleansers we all rely on and gives a simple shopping list of materials which are more environmentally friendly but work just as well.

OTHER FEATURES

Subscribe to their wholesome monthly Newsletter and explore the extensive Links to tips and recipes for home, beauty, and craft projects using 100 per cent natural materials. Article Archives gives access to useful pieces such as Spring Cleaning, Cutting Costs in the Home, and Spend Less Time Doing Household Chores.

Throw away your aerosols. After exploring this site, you will be keen to explore more environmentally friendly ways of cleaning your home. The enormous number of useful, reliable household tips are simply and clearly presented.

www.a2zcarpet.com

a2zcarpet

Overall rating: ★ ★ ★		
Classification: Advice	Readability:	★ ★ ★ ★
Updating: Monthly	Content:	★ ★ ★ ★
Navigation: ★ ★ ★	Speed:	★ ★ ★

US

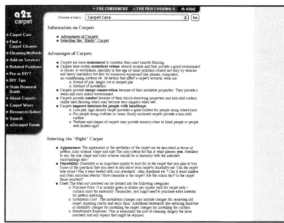

This site, produced by the a2z web and database company, is dedicated to the care of carpets and rugs, and is full of relevant cleaning and maintenance advice. Use the scroll-down menu at the top, or menu bars on the left-hand side of the page to navigate quickly and easily between sections.

SPECIAL FEATURES

Carpet Care Did you know that three to seven strokes of the vacuum cleaner is the optimum number? This, and lots more advice on spot removal, including suggestions on how to know when it's time to clean the whole carpet.

Carpet Cleaning Methods offers advice on the merits of different kinds of professional cleaning, from hot water extraction, to steam cleaning, and which one would best suit your carpet.

Some DIY Tips from selecting a carpet in the first place, to advice on cleaning it yourself.

Interactive Stain Removal Guide gives general advice on removing stains from carpets. There is also a scroll-down box at the top of the page detailing dozens of specific stains. Click to find out how to eradicate them.

Consumer Guide to Oriental Rugs is a simple, enjoyable introduction to oriental carpets, with illustrations and the odd pop quiz thrown in for your interactive amusement.

Divided into five modules covering how rugs are made, design elements, types and value, there is little here for the carpet connoisseur, but it's quite good fun for beginners.

OTHER FEATURES

Use the Forum to ask specific questions about carpets and rugs. It is quite busy, with answers of varying degrees of usefulness. Professional carpet-care companies seem keen to jump in with advice.

An easily navigated site packed with useful information about the care and purchase of carpets.

www.heloise.com
Hints from Heloise

Overall rating: ★ ★ ★

Classification:	Homepage	**Readability:**	★ ★ ★
Updating:	Often	**Content:**	★ ★ ★
Navigation:	★ ★	**Speed:**	★ ★ ★

(US)

Hints from Heloise is an American institution, started by the original Heloise in Honolulu in 1959, and now the dust-free torch is carried by her daughter in newspaper columns, television and radio shows, and a popular column in the American Good Housekeeping magazine. Heloise also hosts a live monthly chat on the magazine's website. Her prodigious output lead People magazine to call her 'the world's best known housekeeper'.

SPECIAL FEATURES

Heloise's Top 10 Hints gives the answers to her most popular queries, such as how to clean drinking glasses made cloudy by the dishwasher, and eliminating odours from rubbish bins and waste disposal units. There is also a section on stopping blue jeans from fading, a preoccupation with the very Texan Heloise.

Stain Removal Calendar supplies a year's worth of stain removal hints. You may find her suggestion for removing chocolate from clothing more useful than the one for getting troublesome clay out of baseball uniforms.

OTHER FEATURES

Recipes & Food Hints includes such delicacies as Texas Caviar which involves black-eyed beans and picante sauce, so perhaps the international shortage of sturgeon isn't quite so terrible after all. Also check out the prize-winning recipe for something called Red Velvet Cake, which resembles nothing so much as a carefully iced placenta. Enjoy!

Heloise signs herself 'your hintologist friend', so perhaps a little less fluff and a little more advice could be reasonably expected from her own homepage.

www.pioneerthinking.com/household.html

Pioneerthinking.com

Overall rating: ★ ★ ★			
Classification:	Ezine	Readability:	★ ★ ★
Updating:	Frequent	Content:	★ ★ ★ ★
Navigation:	★ ★ ★	Speed:	★ ★ ★

CAN

This award-winning site has nothing to do with Laura Ingalls Wilder's Little House on the Prairie, and everything to do with a calm and simple attitude to life. It is crammed with ideas for enjoying a more environmentally friendly, less complicated existence. The site's homepage promises recipes for banana hair smoothies, herbal teas, and homemade ice cream, but we begin on the Home & Family page which offers many quick and cheap ideas to change the way you look at cleaning. It is relatively simple to move from one page to another, though some of the links could be quicker, given that illustrations are relatively scarce and uncomplicated.

SPECIAL FEATURES

Household Cleaning Solutions has lots of down-to-earth suggestions on solving cleaning problems. The Walls section has advice on removing crayon and fingermarks from wallpaper, and also helpful tips on removing soot from walls, an increasingly common problem since the revival in popularity of real fires. Laundry offers straightforward advice, for example on using lemon juice and salt to get rid of mildew stains. Check out the Stain Remover Guide too, an A to Z of stubborn marks and ways to remove them, from beer and blood, through candlewax, Vaseline, and wine. They could also perhaps suggest that, next time, the local Hell's Angels chapter meets at someone else's house.

Homemade Cleaners gives recipes using 'easily available' ingredients to do away with damaging chemicals, though good luck trying to find your local stockist of Neat's-Foot Oil. There are links to homemade cleaning products and household cleaning tips.

Home Repair Tips includes some great, practical suggestions for easier cleaning and decorating. Ideas such as smearing door handles and hinges with petroleum jelly before painting so that any drips or splashes can simply be wiped off when you are finished are good. The suggestion that you clean out nail varnish bottles and fill them with small amounts of paint so that you can perform quick touch ups on scuffs and scratches is slightly less useful.

OTHER FEATURES

Subscribe to their free monthly Newsletter which is available to view online. You can also email this useful domestic site to a grubby but eco-conscious friend.

A wholesome site with the tone of a sort of homemade, mini Reader's Digest. Worth looking at though for the plethora of practical tips.

www.tipztime.com
Tipztime

Overall rating: ★ ★ ★			
Classification:	Homepage	Readability:	★ ★ ★
Updating:	Daily	Content:	★ ★ ★ ★
Navigation:	★ ★ ★	Speed:	★ ★ ★

US

In 1997, American 'mom', Wendy Shepherd, set up this site as a personal homepage with a domestic slant. She was inundated with household tips from family and friends, and it blossomed into this promising repository of tips, gardening advice, crafts ideas and domestic lore. It is a little bitty in parts, but there is some useful advice to be found here nonetheless. Use the scroll-down Tips Menu at the bottom of the page to select an area that interests you.

SPECIAL FEATURES

Household Tips includes Money Savers which brings up many useful pages, including Cleaners, Shopping, and Home. Use the menu bar at the left of the page to select a more specific interest. For example, Living Room brings up several tips, including Frames, which offers the excellent suggestion of sticking small pieces of rubber to the back of pictures to stop them marking walls or slipping and becoming crooked.

Christmas Tips contains some useful advice, including buying stocking fillers in Back to School sales. The suggestion of icing a Pop Tart with someone's name to create an unusual place setting is perhaps less useful.

OTHER FEATURES

Sign up to TipzTime's free monthly newsletter for advice from the cutting edge of housekeeping.

A rather quaint little site, but useful nonetheless.

OTHER SITES OF INTEREST

Don't forget sites in the Antiques and Architectural Salvage chapter for specific advice on cleaning older pieces, such as:

BBC Online Antiques on the Web
www.bbc.co.uk/antiques

British Antique Furniture Restorers' Association
www.bafra.org.uk

LAPADA
www.lapada.co.uk

All Things Frugal
www.allthingsfrugal.com

This is home to an American phenomenon, The Pennypincher ezine and Tightwad Tidbits Daily, to which you can subscribe for free if you should wish to. It is a no-frills site which encourages economy at every turn. Indeed, with advice on using powdered eggs and milk in cooking and suggestions that you can cut down on your use of flour by removing two tablespoons for every cup used in a recipe, you might almost imagine that there was still a war on and hear Dame Vera Lynn warbling about white cliffs in the background. Their idea of a treasure hunt is Dumpster Diving – that's rummaging around in a skip to you and I. They helpfully suggest taking with you a long stick, a headlamp for nocturnal explorations and antibacterial hand lotion for obvious reasons. An amusing curiosity really, and of practical use only to those who view frugality as a sort of competitive sport.

The New Homemaker
www.newhomemaker.com

A very folksy American site with rather too much proselytising about the horrors of the working mother. Get past the Stepford Wife overtones though, as the Clean and Organized section includes quite a good Forum for general household enquiries, and some useful Links to other sites. Ask the Miserly Mom is worth a look for sensible money-saving tips.

learning

Television shows make it all look so easy: take ten pounds and ten minutes, and transform your bedsit into a boudoir. Of course, real life isn't quite so simple, and for many of us our imagination outstrips our competence. As a result, evening classes and full-time courses across the country are jammed with people seizing the opportunity to brush up on some basic skills before they tackle major projects.

If the idea of dragging yourself out on a rainy Monday evening to spend a couple of hours in a draughty hall learning the finer principles of rag rolling doesn't appeal, the internet provides some welcome alternatives.

Some establishments allow prospective students to peruse their curriculum online, perhaps view a sample lesson or two, and some offer more extensive support. Bulletin boards, chat rooms, and even online tutorials create a sense of 'belonging' for the distance learner, and the more multi-media savvy institutions are starting to provide these. Unfortunately, in some cases, such ambitious plans are somewhat let down by old-fashioned-looking and poorly designed websites, which is unfortunate for institutions seeking to encourage an aesthetic sense.

www.klc.co.uk
KLC School

Overall rating: ★ ★ ★ ★ ★

Classification:	Education	Readability:	★ ★ ★ ★ ★
Updating:	Annually	Content:	★ ★ ★ ★
Navigation:	★ ★ ★ ★	Speed:	★ ★ ★ ★

UK

Over the past 20 years, KLC has gained an excellent reputation in the decorating trade for the high standards of its professional training. Through on-site and distance learning programmes, its students receive either a thorough vocational training, or gain the skills and confidence to take a more professional approach to decorating their own homes. If you're about to tackle a large decorating project yourself, it's worth thinking about how much money you can save in the long term if you really know what you're doing. When it comes to interior design projects, mistakes can be very expensive.

The KLC site is quick, clear, and simple to use. The company sees its website as an important part of its public face, and it's about to play an even bigger part in their training operation. They plan to include an events and exhibitions page, a chatroom and bulletin board for students, and even online tutorials. While this will be useful for all students, it will be particularly beneficial for students taking part in their distance-learning programmes.

SPECIAL FEATURES

Full-Time Training at KLC describes the company's intensive, highly vocational courses. All classes require 10am-4pm attendance every week day, and courses range from the 10-week Certificate, to the one-year Advanced Diploma in Interior Design. Teaching is based around design projects, and is supremely practical, with work experience in the trade encouraged. They claim that 90 per cent of students go on to full-time employment.

Short/Part Time Courses include specialist introductory courses designed to further an interest or polish an already existing skill. Examples are Antiques in Interiors, Sketching Workshop, and Professional Presentation.

Open Learning Courses encourages contact with KLC's offices in London's Chelsea Harbour. On enrolment, students are assigned a personal tutor whom they can contact via telephone, fax, or email five days a week. Home Study Networking Days allow students to visit the school to attend seminars on specialist subjects and meet other students and tutors.

OTHER FEATURES

KLC Open Learning Association Enrolled students are automatically members of this club, which entitles them to discounts on some other KLC courses, and on books and materials. The association also gives an award to the home-study student who achieves the most in the year.

An elegant, informative site which reflects this company's enthusiasm for and commitment to good design. The moves to make the site more interactive with a chatroom and online tutorials promise to make it even better.

www.kenturnerflowerschool.com
Kenneth Turner Flower School

Overall rating: ★ ★ ★ ★

Classification:	Education	**Readability:**	★ ★ ★ ★
Updating:	Varies	**Content:**	★ ★ ★ ★
Navigation:	★ ★ ★	**Speed:**	★ ★ ★ ★

UK 🔒

Ken Turner grew up in Ireland and trained in horticulture and landscape design before working for Pulbrook & Gould, the smart society florist. Since then, he has developed his own distictive English Country House style. There's nothing stuffy about his designs, however. They're luxurious, abundant, and witty, rather like their inventor. He was one of the first to use shells, lichen, pebbles, fruit, and vegetables in arrangements, and to transform dried flower arrangements from tired and dusty phantoms of the real thing, into chic decorative objects in themselves.

The Flower School's website is characteristically smart and beautifully illustrated. Move around by clicking on the oak leaf icons on the left of the screen.

SPECIAL FEATURES

Course Calendar details the enticing list of classes run by Ken Turner's London Flower School. There's an imaginative selection. Chose from Styling for Dinner Parties, Fashionable Flowers, if your taste is more relaxed than full-blown, and seasonal specials such as Christmas Table Decoration and Autumn Weddings. Some courses are timed to coincide with Chelsea and Hampton Court Flower Shows, so out-of-town visitors can include a little flower play in their trip. Prices are steep (about £200 for a day's course and £900 for a week's intensive training), but you do get lunch, an apron, a bag, a pencil, a pad, and pair of flower snips thrown in.

OTHER FEATURES

KT Shop directs web surfers to telephone Turner's Mayfair shop to discuss flower arrangements with his staff. He misses a trick here; as well as fabulous flowers, Mr Turner also makes deliciously scented candles, smart candlesticks, and holders. It seems a pity that these eminently postable items aren't included on this page.

KT Books If £200 for a day's flower wrangling is a little out of your reach, order one of KT's ravishingly beautiful books on 'floral art' from this page.

A characteristically elegant site which makes you want to rush out into the garden and plunder the flower bed. It's a pity the KT Shop section is so limited though.

www.rhodec.com
RHODEC International

Overall rating: ★★★★			
Classification: Education		**Readability:**	★★★★
Updating: Varies		**Content:**	★★★★★
Navigation: ★★★★		**Speed:**	★★★★

UK

RHODEC International teaches competitively priced introductory and professional interior design courses by distance-learning, which is great for those who want or need to continue working to finance their study. It's accredited by the ODLQC, the Open and Distance Learning Quality Council, and the standard of training is high. Serious students can even go on to convert their Diploma into a Bachelor of Arts degree if they wish. The site is very easy to use. Use the menu bar on the left to zip between sections or get back to the homepage. You can also download the whole prospectus or catalogue and enrol online via a secure server if you want to pay by credit card. The design of the site, however, could be a little more inspirational given the content of the course.

SPECIAL FEATURES

List of Subjects From Materials to History of Design, Draughtsmanship to Colour and Furniture, check on the text to see a sample illustration and in some cases the entire course manual.

Online Diploma Course Students can complete the entire Diploma via the internet at a saving of £300 on the normal course fee.

Associate Diploma Course A one-year course divided into 12 detailed lessons with assignments. The 32 worksheets run to 160,000 words with 100 illustrations, and cover the basics of design history, materials, sample boards, estimates and professional practice. If you enjoy the course enough to want to do the two- to three-year Diploma Course, credits can be carried over and there is a discount on the total course fee. The Diploma Course aims to train students to a high professional standard and can be converted into a full Bachelor of Arts degree with London Guildhall University.

OTHER FEATURES

Course Preview allows customers to 'try before you buy' with 50,000 words of course text and 200 photographs from the course materials for £15.

Students Tell Us is a predictably laudatory section with testimonials from former students across the world. The Graduate Survey also demonstrates a high level of customer satisfaction, with 91 per cent of recent graduates saying they had put their skills to practical use, and 90 per cent saying that the Diploma had helped them with their career.

Bulletin Board After all the gloss, it's strangely reassuring to see that the board is just as catty and full of poor spelling as any other.

The site is very accessible and enthusiastically written. The design lets it down a little, and could do with an overhaul to make it look a little fresher and more current.

www.anniesloan.com
Annie Sloan School of Decoration

Overall rating: ★ ★ ★			
Classification: Business		**Readability:**	★ ★ ★ ★
Updating: Varies		**Content:**	★ ★ ★ ★
Navigation:	★ ★ ★ ★	**Speed:**	★ ★ ★ ★

UK

If you thought paint effects were passé, Annie Sloan is the woman to convince you otherwise. In over 20 years of working as a decorator and teacher, she has created and inspired stylish interiors across the world. This website gives her Oxford shop, Practical Style, a presence on the internet, providing a catalogue of her many products and classes. The site is luxuriously illustrated with Annie Sloan's interiors and products, which doesn't seem to slow down its speed.

SPECIAL FEATURES

Courses are taught in a room above the shop with no more than eight students in each class. A light lunch is provided and they can provide recommendations of places to stay if you're coming from out of town. Chose from How to Paint Furniture, Decorative Gilding, and Modern Paint Effects; in most cases ten different techniques are taught each day and students get to take samples of their work home with them. Unfortunately, you have to email for more detailed course information, dates, and prices; it would be good to have them available online.

Paint & Pigments is a highly tempting section. Enticing shots of Annie Sloan's fabulous selection of paints, pigments, and materials bring would inspire even the least creative among us to pull on some overalls. Her eight colour ranges cover a broad colour and style spectrum, from

Traditional to Vibrant, Pearlized to Sparkle. Order online via a secure site.

OTHER FEATURES

Interiors Gallery shows photographs from some of her books with links to order the paints and other products used in the pictures. If you can't see the porcelain paint through the aluminium leaf trees, use the Search facility which opens up quickly on a separate window so you don't have to interrupt your browsing.

A stylish site which provides a good introduction to Annie Sloan's extensive range of innovative products. It would be improved, however, with more specific information on courses and events.

www.cambridgefinefurnishings.co.uk
Cambridge Fine Furnishings

Overall rating: ★ ★ ★			
Classification:	Education	**Readability:**	★ ★ ★
Updating:	Varies	**Content:**	★ ★ ★ ★
Navigation:	★ ★ ★ ★	**Speed:**	★ ★ ★ ★

UK

Set in a 17th century stable block, Stanford Hall is a suitably elegant place to learn how to create elegant soft furnishings. Whether you want to revamp your own living room or make a living revamping the living rooms of others, there should be something to interest you here. This straightforward site is packed with details of their many courses, but it could perhaps do with some inspirational photographs to get the creative juices flowing.

SPECIAL FEATURES

Workshops Use the pull-down menu at the top of the page to select a workshop from the extensive selection. These classes include a four-day course in making loose covers, to which students are asked to bring a chair they wish to cover and the fabric with which to cover it, a day's cushion making when you can make two yourself and 'learn the art of cushion placement', and an Advanced Tassels class which has been extended to three days as, after the two-day course, students apparently enjoyed themselves so much they didn't want to go home.

Certificate/Diploma These longer courses of two to three weeks are made up of a selection of the shorter Workshops.

OTHER FEATURES

Latest News keeps crafty types up to date with new courses

on offer, such as millinery and machine quilting, and the credentials of instructors who teach them. There's nothing here you can't discover elsewhere, which is rather a shame as it would be a good opportunity to breathe a little life into what is a rather dry site.

An impressively broad curriculum which is let down by its presentation. An effort to make this site more visually arresting without slowing it down would be very welcome.

www.inchbald.co.uk
Inchbald School of Design

Overall rating: ★ ★ ★			
Classification:	Education	**Readability:**	★ ★ ★
Updating:	Varies	**Content:**	★ ★ ★
Navigation:	★ ★	**Speed:**	★ ★ ★ ★

UK

The Inchbald School of Design's logo throbs on the lower-right of their homepage, enticing you to enter. To enter the site, you're informed, you need to have the latest Flash plug-in and the site offers you the ability to download this. Unusually, however, it doesn't offer a non-flash version of the site. Once inside, there is a scrolling menu moving left to right that is tricky to navigate and not very clear. The print is quite small and faint grey-blue on white which, coupled with the moving graphics, combines to induce a feeling of seasickness in the reader.

The overall impression left by this site is that the Inchbald, realising that they were one of the country's leading suppliers of design education, thought they needed a graphically challenging site. Unfortunately, it's graphic-heavy and content-lite.

SPECIAL FEATURES

Interior Design The Inchbald's courses cover the whole spectrum, from the 15-week Certificate in Interior Decoration at a handsome £6,000, to the Master of Arts degree validated by the University of Wales at considerably more. Courses also include a One-Year Diploma, a One Year Diploma with Advanced Studies and an Advanced Level Diploma.

What's New includes a Newsletter and useful Links to many museums and decorative arts societies across the world.

Other Courses For those who want the prestige and rigour of Inchbald training without shelling out thousands of pounds for the privilege, their Home Study Course accredited by the National Extension College is a snip at £550. It is aimed at helping students with design projects for their own home, or to provide a basis for further study. Successful completion of the course leads to the Foundation Course Design Certificate.

A rather off-putting site from this eminent design school. It is cold and needlessly 'tricksy', with irritating graphics which add nothing to the appeal of the site.

www.regentacademy.com
Regent Academy

Overall rating: ★ ★ ★			
Classification:	Education	**Readability:**	★ ★ ★ ★
Updating:	Annually	**Content:**	★ ★ ★
Navigation:	★ ★	**Speed:**	★ ★ ★ ★

UK

Regent Academy runs many successful art and design courses to which this site offers a comprehensive introduction. The site is a little old fashioned in its design and annoyingly sensitive to the cursor. Each time it was tested, merely placing the cursor over a highlighted area was sufficient to switch between pages. A frustrating process, and one which led to much irritation in the reviewing of this site.

Much is made of prices being discounted for booking over the internet, but it is not made clear what the standard price would be.

SPECIAL FEATURES

Successful Interior Design provides tips and advice for beginners wanting to transform their homes. This course represents between 150 and 200 hours work divided into 25 lessons, from paint finishes to transforming loft rooms. The package includes audio and videotapes, and even a set of watercolour paints to help you with your designs. Once you've completed this course, you're eligible for a City & Guilds Certificate.

Professional Interior Design builds on the first course and allows students to progress to a professional level, with advice on setting up your own consultancy, and the particular challenges of designing for homes, hotels, bars, restaurants, and offices. Taught in 10 modules, the package includes video and audio tapes on job hunting and working from home. Completion of the course allows students to qualify for an Advanced City & Guilds Certificate.

Discover Decorative Paint Effects teaches a wide range of skills for transforming walls and furniture. The ubiquitous ragging, stippling, and combing are covered, as well as more adventurous finishes such as granite and tortoiseshell.

Master Soft Furnishings aims to 'help give your home a unique personality'. You should also learn how to create window treatments, bed furnishings, cushion covers and lampshades.

OTHER FEATURES

Understanding Antiques aims to encourage confidence in new collectors. Written by Sotheby's experts, including David Battie of Antiques Roadshow fame, you need never again quake in the face of a flea market, or be a bashful bidder at auction. Students completing the course are eligible for a City & Guilds Certificate in the History of English Furniture.

Attendance Courses in Successful Interior Design are taught over 16 evenings at the Regent Academy's London headquarters. One-week Interior Design and Antiques courses are also taught.

Free Advisory Service offers enrolled students a free phone number to call for help and advice with their projects.

A somewhat uninspiring site which conveys most of the relevant information but with little panache. If the Regent Academy feel that their courses can compete with the many others out there, then their website should be able to hold its own too.

www.spaceclearing.com
The Feng Shui Art of Space Clearing

Overall rating: ★ ★ ★			
Classification: Education		**Readability:**	★ ★ ★
Updating: Varies		**Content:**	★ ★ ★ ★
Navigation:	★ ★ ★ ★	**Speed:**	★ ★ ★

UK

Space clearing is the branch of Feng Shui that Karen Kingston has made her own. The sensible premise that surrounding yourself with junk prevents you from living a creative, happy and full life has made her popular with sceptics as well as with Feng Shui devotees. The site of her Space Clearing company suggests you can improve your energy flow by altering building design, furniture placement, and colour schemes. A highly motivational speaker, there's also a frequently updated calendar to her talks and workshops.

The site is soothingly pink and swift. The glow rather disappears, however, when you realise you can't order goods or courses online. Instead, you're invited to print out a form and snail mail your order to them or, worse, email your credit card details. Call me spiritually unevolved, but I still believe there are some bad people out there who might take advantage of my financial information if I include it in a vulnerable little email.

SPECIAL FEATURES

Workshops details Ms Kingston's dizzying international schedule, covering the United Kingdom, the rest of Europe, North America, and the East. There's an email link so that you can book Ms Kingston for a private consultation if you should wish to. Introductory one-day courses start at £75.

Products Spaceclearing.com has the clear intention of helping you to divest yourself of unwanted clutter, which seems to include a hefty wedge of cash. To aid you in your quest to spiritual harmony, they offer a Balinese Empress bell for £200, and an ordinary Balinese bell for a mere £90. Breathe deeply; the incense is only £8.

Books The chapter on streamlining your life in Karen Kingston's highly successful book, Creating Sacred Space With Feng Shui, was so popular that she expanded it into a book on its own, Clear Your Clutter With Feng Shui. A clearly written and inspirational work, it's pleasingly short so won't contribute to the chaos of your bookshelves.

Ask Karen Kingston is the section where the guru herself answers the 'most interesting' of the many questions she is sent each month. These include what to do when your hands get sore from too much clapping to banish stale energy (use hand cream apparently), and the likely toxicity of flower petal baths.

OTHER FEATURES

Readers' Letters Evangelical students of the Kingston method enthuse about the beneficial effects of Space Clearing in their lives. Useless husbands, unwanted wedding presents, and even cellulite are banished on the road to nirvana.

Links to sites on colon cleansing (like nanny, Ms Kingston likes her charges to be clean all over), rebirthing and geopathic stress.

Miss Kingston elevates the simple act of taking the rubbish out to a spiritual act. Her site is appropriately clean and simple to navigate, but would be greatly improved by supplying a secure link for ordering products.

OTHER SITES OF INTEREST

Don''t forget sites in the Antiques and Architectural Salvage chapter such as:

Christies
www.christie.com

Sothebys
www. sothebys.com

When looking for an education in antiques:

City & Guilds
www.city-and-guilds.co.uk
City & Guilds is the leading provider of vocational qualifications in the United Kingdom with over 400 courses covering nearly every occupation you can imagine. Whether you want to change your career or simply learn a new skill, their thorough and reasonably-priced courses are a good place to start. Perhaps because of the sheer number of classes on offer, the site is somewhat labyrinthine. An attempt to use the search facility to find courses on soft furnishings inexplicably brought up a reference to Medals

for Excellence in Photography. Better to click on the City & Guilds logo and go to the Our Qualifications section. Then use the pull-down menu to view a list of subjects and click into Creative Arts, Crafts & Leisure Pursuits which brings up a selection of courses including Basic Soft Furnishings & Upholstery, Introduction to Home Interior Design, and Furniture Restoration. Send an email to discover local teaching centres; our enquiry yielded a reply within two hours.

Sheffield School of Interior Design
www.sheffield.edu.com
This American school runs multi-media education programmes in interior design and claims to have trained more people in design and decoration than any other school in the world. Even after viewing a free lesson on furniture layout, British students may not be interested in taking their courses, but this is a worthwhile site nonetheless. Check out the Designer Monthly page which has lots of great, practical tips, the Question & Answer Section for the Anxious Decorator, and the Room of the Month for a little transatlantic inspiration.

Chapter 08

miscellany

Just as a meal made up of left-overs is often the most appetising, so the sites included in this chapter – the ones that didn't quite fit in anywhere else – are some of the most useful on the web.

There are included here many practical sites aimed at householders, some of which, I admit, are rather dry. Still, the more you know the more you save, and the more you save the more you have to spend. The fewer mistakes you make in finding your mortgage, fixing up your improvement loan, or obtaining home insurance, the more money you'll have left over to fritter, sorry invest, in that heavenly sofa or that to-swoon-for bed linen.

Included here too are some excellent sites which reflect the current interest in renovating old houses sensitively and authentically. The information you need to bring an old building back to life has never been more readily available. And if you don't happen to have your own piece of historic Britain, the web provides one of the least Volvo-intensive ways of finding one too. You can explore ruined chapels, decrepit watertowers, and run-down oast houses without even getting your wellies wet.

www.o8oo4homes.com

o8oo4homes.com

Overall rating: ★ ★ ★ ★

Classification:	Company	Readability:	★ ★ ★ ★ ★
Updating:	Daily	Content:	★ ★ ★ ★ ★
Navigation:	★ ★ ★	Speed:	★ ★ ★ ★

UK

This site is aimed primarily at people wishing to buy, sell or let a home, but if you're not in that position there are still plenty of other reasons to drop by. The site covers decorating, finance, and legal matters with insight, sophistication, and amazingly, the occasional outburst of wit. The site is laid out in an attractive and approachable manner, is easy to navigate, and is brimming with useful information.

SPECIAL FEATURES

Propertysearch@o8oo4homes.com Search their database of over 170,000 homes to buy or rent, including the special section on newly-built houses. The search can be as general or specific as you wish to make it. Once you select a property, More Info, on the right, allows you to access expansive details on the property's location.

Finance@o8oo4homes.com Look here for up-to-date advice on the mortgage and insurance markets. Down the right-hand side of the page, there is a useful summary of features. Can I Afford It? is a simple calculator which works out the monthly repayment on a particular loan amount at a proposed rate of interest.

Living@o8oo4homes.com is a lively section, constantly updated, and with a broader appeal than most sites of this type. At the time of writing, features included ones on

hunting for student accommodation, moving to the UK from abroad, building timber kit houses in 48 hours, and dealing with nightmare neighbours. Property analyst John Wriglesworth hosts The House Doctor page and makes admirable sense of the complicated house market. Your Letters provides detailed and authoritative answers to readers' house-related problems. Ask the Experts is the place to look to get the answers to common problems from legal, property, mortgage and design aficionados.

Interiors@o8oo4homes.com Just glancing at this section has the potential to increase the value of your home. Click on Features to access solid information on decorating, upholstery, discovering the history of your home and working with a designer. Check out Our House for makeover features on real homes; drag the cursor over the sublimely lovely image before you to see the midden it was before. Shopping has good Buying Guide information, New Products reviews, and an excellent Source Book. Designers has often irreverent interviews with top designers such as Nicholas Haslam, John Rocha, and Robin Anderson. Use the drop-down menu at the top of the page for a quick burst of retail therapy.

A superlative site, brimming with clearly presented and well written information. The place to go to keep your finger on the property pulse.

www.architecture.com

RIBA

Overall rating: ★ ★ ★ ★			
Classification:	Professional	**Readability:**	★ ★ ★ ★
Updating:	Regularly	**Content:**	★ ★ ★ ★
Navigation:	★ ★ ★ ★	**Speed:**	★ ★ ★

UK

This is the site of the Royal Institute of British Architects and it contains more than a quarter of a million pages of information on architecture, architects and the association itself. Although it is essentially aimed at the professionals, the site is clear and approachable to the interested lay person, with links to over 800 sites. Use the menu down the left-hand side of the page to navigate between sections.

SPECIAL FEATURES

Find an Architect will help you find the right person for your project, no matter how small. Click on 103 Things Architects Do for a dazzlingly comprehensive survey of the services they provide. And be prepared, it's a whole lot more than creating pretty designs and writing in funky capital letters.

RIBA Directory of Practices should be your first stop if you are planning a building project. Click on UK Directory, and then use the drop-down menu to select your county. You can further refine your search by entering your town, the type of job, and the proposed budget. When you click on a particular architect, a detailed description of their practice will appear in a pop-up window. Small Work & Domestic Projects gives a good introduction to what to expect if you've never used an architect before.

OTHER FEATURES

The RIBA Bookshop gives access to an extensive range of architecture and design books, including frequently updated special offers, available from their shops or via a secure server online.

If you have never used an architect before, this site will give you an idea of what to expect and how to go about it.

www.heritage.co.uk/georgian
The Georgian Group

Overall rating: ★ ★ ★ ★			
Classification:	Society	Readability:	★ ★ ★ ★
Updating:	Regularly	Content:	★ ★ ★ ★
Navigation:	★ ★ ★	Speed:	★ ★ ★

UK

The Georgian group was founded in 1937 to save Georgian buildings, monuments, parks, and gardens from destruction or disfigurement. In the early days, in a wonderful demonstration of noblesse oblige, writer Nancy Mitford offered to chain herself, naked, to the railings of a threatened London terrace. They did not take her up on her offer. Since then they have successfully campaigned to stem the tide of demolitions without recourse to nudity. If you are fortunate enough to own a Georgian house, or are simply interested in Georgian architecture and history, this site is a wonderful resource. Scroll down to the bottom of the homepage to see the links to the site's different sections.

SPECIAL FEATURES

Of Interest to Members gives details of exhibitions, London's annual Open House days when visitors can explore over 450 buildings normally closed to the public, guided visits, and lectures. This is the section where new books are reviewed and you can find information on other interesting subjects, such as recordings of Georgian music.

Georgian Group Forthcoming Events is the place to look if you want to learn more about the period. The members' study days are wide-ranging and justifiably popular. Enjoy tours of private houses, private views of exhibitions, and guided walks around historically interesting areas. Many of the events are centred on London, but there are numerous activities spread out across the country too. At the time of writing, highly tempting events in Sussex, Yorkshire, Hampshire, Lancashire, and Cumbria were listed.

Georgian Group Publications is home to their many excellent and inexpensive Advisory Leaflets aimed at the Georgian home-owner. These contain a brief but authoritative history of the styles of the period, as well as practical guidelines for authentic renovation. They are illustrated, contain useful reference sections, and cover many areas, including Windows, Paint Colour, Wallpaper, Curtains and Blinds, Fireplaces and Stonework.

OTHER FEATURES

To find out about all the latest Georgian Group projects and campaigns, go to Casework Report.

A straightforward site containing much useful information for those who are renovating Georgian houses – or for those who only wish they were.

www.spab.org.uk
Society for the Protection of Ancient Buildings

Overall rating: ★ ★ ★ ★			
Classification:	Society	**Readability:**	★ ★ ★ ★ ★
Updating:	Regularly	**Content:**	★ ★ ★ ★ ★
Navigation:	★ ★ ★ ★	**Speed:**	★ ★ ★ ★

UK

The Society for the Protection of Ancient Buildings (SPAB) was founded by William Morris in 1877 to combat the destructive 'restoration' of mediaeval buildings by over-enthusiastic Victorian architects. It is now an influential pressure group which saves important buildings from demolition, decay, and damage. Although many of their members are conservation practitioners, lots of their work is also carried out by sympathetic volunteers. SPAB offers advice on every aspect of repairing old buildings, promoting traditional materials and skills, modern technical issues, regulations, and materials.

SPECIAL FEATURES

Noticeboard Click on Events to find out about courses and lectures. Many of them are aimed at professionals, but there is a good selection of more general classes and talks. Of particular note is the Homeowners' Course, a two-day seminar held several times a year and in different parts of the country, which encourages sympathetic renovation and allows similarly-minded people to swap experiences and advice.

Publications & Advice gives details of their selection of Technical Pamphlets and Information Sheets, as well as other recommended reading. There is no facility to order online or by credit card over the phone – the cheque has to be in the post. The Society also runs an over-the-phone

advisory service on weekday mornings. Look Before You Leap is a must-read feature, particularly if you are the kind of person who gets misty eyed at the sight of peeling plaster and rustic paintwork.

Membership costs from £10, and forms can be downloaded and opened using Adobe Acrobat. Members receive a quarterly newsletter, and have exclusive access to the Properties List of dilapidated buildings in need of a saviour. Their 13 Regional Groups meet regularly; find one near you.

Friendly, practical, and thoughtful, this site is filled with useful information. If you own an architecturally important house, or you'd just like to help renovate one, this site has lots to interest you.

www.upmystreet.com			
UpMyStreet.com			
Overall rating: ★ ★ ★ ★ ★			
Classification: Information		**Readability:**	★ ★ ★ ★ ★
Updating: Monthly		**Content:**	★ ★ ★ ★ ★
Navigation: ★ ★ ★ ★		**Speed:**	★ ★ ★ ★
UK			

www.yourmortgage.co.uk			
Your Mortgage			
Overall rating: ★ ★ ★ ★			
Classification: Magazine		**Readability:**	★ ★ ★ ★ ★
Updating: Monthly		**Content:**	★ ★ ★ ★
Navigation: ★ ★ ★ ★ ★		**Speed:**	★ ★ ★ ★
UK			

In the creation of this book, we trawled through thousands of sites to select the best. It was a real delight to come across sites that exploited the medium to provide a service which simply could not have existed without the advent of the net. This award-winning site makes brilliant use of the web to pick and probe at the latest published statistics about where you live – or where you'd like to live. Within seconds, you have access to a wealth of information it would have taken you days to gather only a few short years ago.

SPECIAL FEATURES

Go Start by feeding your postcode into the box on the left-hand side of the homepage. This will bring up a graph of property prices in your area against the national average. You can then compare your area with another part of the country, or even another part of the city if you're an urban creature. You can make your search more detailed by comparing up to four other kinds of data, such as a specific kind of house, GCSE results, crime clear up rates, and unemployment. Use the menu at the bottom of the page to go to Postcode Profile, and discover more information about demographics, housing, leisure, food, and drink for your chosen area. You can also use Find My Nearest ... for shops, health services, utilities, education, and more, with precise distances from your door ...

A wonderful site – don't move house without it!

Moving house comes third only to death and divorce in the league table of life's most stressful experiences, so anything that makes it less fraught is to be welcomed. Your Mortgage magazine's website is an exemplary exercise in clarity, providing current, accessible information which you don't need a degree in finance to understand. Use the menu along the top and left-hand side of the homepage to move around. Links to other areas of the site remain visible whatever page you're on, so it's a breeze to navigate.

SPECIAL FEATURES

Find a Mortgage First-time buyers should start with The Mortgage Process, a lucid introduction to the whole, tension-filled process. If you already know what type of mortgage you're after, click on Search the Latest Mortgages for up-to-date information. If you find it all simply too confusing, and the idea of wading through hundreds of different mortgages is about as appealing as an estate agents' convention, go directly to Mortgage Wizard which gives a succinct survey of current mortgage offers.

House Prices Find out how much your house, or the one you are thinking of buying, will be worth in five years' time. Feed in the postcode and the value of the house, and results appear in an easy-to-understand graph. When we tried it out, the graph gave exactly the same value as a local surveyor had given us a month earlier, so we can vouch for its accuracy.

Buying & Selling Your Home The Step-by-Step guide is very easy to follow, if a little simplistic. For more comprehensive information, click on Buying or Selling.

Extra Costs details the things we often forget about in our rush to buy the perfect curtains for a new home. It provides a good indication of just how much conveyancing, contents insurance, and stamp duty are likely to cost. There are also links to property and lender websites.

Checklists includes lots of PDF lists and a link to download Acrobat Reader in order to print them out. Viewing Checklist will help you remember what you've seen in the dizzying rush to find the perfect house. The Contents and Costs Checklists are good too.

News & Editorial Each month there are new features on the latest lending and borrowing trends. At the time of writing, these covered a broad range of subjects, from buying homes online, to the pros and cons of buy-to-let mortgages.

OTHER FEATURES

The section on Life Assurance includes a free service, in conjunction with Direct Life & Pensions, to provide you with a quotation after searching a panel of leading insurers. The Jargon Monitor at the top of the page provides a blissfully clear glossary for those lost in the financial maze of home buying.

If you're buying or selling your house, this site is a must-see. It's so full of useful information, you could lower your blood pressure just by logging on.

www.fmb.org.uk
BRIX

Overall rating: ★ ★ ★			
Classification:	Trade	**Readability:**	★ ★ ★
Updating:	Monthly	**Content:**	★ ★ ★
Navigation:	★ ★ ★ ★	**Speed:**	★ ★ ★

UK

The Builders' Resource and Information Exchange is the website serving the 15,000 members of the Federation of Master Builders and their customers. Although the site is predominantly aimed at the trade, there are several sections offering clear advice and recommendations for homeowners. The Federation has been criticised in the past for lacking teeth, particularly in the area of new build housing, but the information here is sound. Navigate by clicking on the menus down the left- and right-hand site of the page, or by clicking on the thumbnails in the middle.

SPECIAL FEATURES

Find a Builder is the most useful part of the site for homeowners. The pull-down menu covers many trades, from electrical contractors, plasterers, roofers, scaffolders, to heating engineers, painters, and decorators, bricklayers and carpenters. Fill in your postcode and a list of recommended workers will appear, with their websites if they have them. You can then fill in a form, describing the work you want doing in up to 700 words, your preferred start date, budget, and contact details. How it Works has a wordy disclaimer about the Federation not being responsible if, after receiving your 700-word essay, their members fail to contact you.

For Consumers provides helpful suggestions in Steer Clear of Cowboys to prevent yourself being corralled by a dodgy dealer. Simple Forms of Contract advises on the legal aspect of engaging a trades person. Click on The MasterBond Warranty Scheme to find out how you can insure yourself against disaster. A £5,000 job can be covered for £75, which includes a conciliation and arbitration service if your relationship with your contractor degenerates to such a state that you're both throwing all of the tools out of the toolbox.

OTHER FEATURES

The site offers a good selection of links to building-related services. Home & Garden, Architecture, and Property Directories are particularly good.

A well-constructed site which offers a useful service to the consumer. If you are considering work on your house, this is a good place to start.

www.savebritainsheritage.org
Save Britain's Heritage

Overall rating: ★ ★ ★			
Classification:	Campaign	Readability:	★ ★ ★ ★
Updating:	Monthly	Content:	★ ★ ★ ★ ★
Navigation:	★ ★ ★ ★	Speed:	★ ★ ★

UK R

SAVE was created in 1975 by a group of historians, architects, planners, and journalists who wanted to protect architecturally important buildings from the wrecking ball. Since then, they have campaigned to save country houses, redundant churches and chapels, mills, cottages, railway stations, and even asylums. If you are the kind of person who spent your childhood nursing baby birds back to health in a shoe box, and you fancy a bigger challenge, this site may just contain the perfect project for you. Use the menu at the top of the page to navigate between sections.

SPECIAL FEATURES

Buildings At Risk is the heart of this site. It is enthusiastic and positive in tone, and the links on the left give lots of information on repairing houses, obtaining loans and grants and the role of local authorities. Click on Examples to go to details of the latest properties to be placed on the register in Buildings of the Month. If you want to see more properties and have subscribed (see Join), click on Access the Register.

Join SAVE for £15 a year. This entitles you to two newsletters a year and a 20 per cent discount on publications, as well as the opportunity of making a most welcome contribution to their campaign funds.

Publications The annual Catalogue of Buildings at Risk is available to non-members for £10 and contains over 100 properties in need of rescuing all over England and Wales. You can also buy special reports on Industrial Buildings, Farm Buildings, and numerous booklets on specific campaigns.

OTHER FEATURES

News gives up-to-date information on current projects as well as associated pieces on the planning and grants. The site also has comprehensive Links for anyone interested in period properties.

Lots of advice for those interested in finding an historic building to renovate, as well as practical help for those who already own one. Do not surf this site if you fall in love easily or suffer from a rescue complex. It could end up costing you a lot of money.

www.victorian-society.org.uk
The Victorian Society

Overall rating: ★ ★ ★			
Classification:	Society	**Readability:**	★ ★
Updating:	Regularly	**Content:**	★ ★ ★ ★ ★
Navigation:	★ ★ ★ ★	**Speed:**	★ ★ ★

UK

If you feel you are due for an eye test, but don't have time to visit the optician, visit this site instead. If you can read it without generating a pounding head and crow's feet to rival Dot Cotton's, then you have most excellent eyesight indeed. This highly-informative site is rather let down by its frustrating design, but if you have even a passing interest in Victorian and Edwardian architecture then persevere. It will turn you into a devotee.

SPECIAL FEATURES

Events is a comprehensive guide to the Society's educational programme, access to which is mostly limited to members. The selection is imaginative and varied. Whether your taste is a one-day tour of Aldershot Army Camp, a week's tour of the Manor Houses of the Prussian Junkers in Potsdam, or even A Pod With a View, an intriguing talk on some of London's finest Victorian and Edwardian architecture from the uniquely Twenty-First Century perspective of the London Eye, there is bound to be something here to tempt you.

Advice to Home Owners Click on Care for Victorian Houses for an introduction to the Society's popular renovation guides, including individual pamphlets on those skills at which the Victorians excelled: Interior Mouldings, Cast Iron, Brickwork and Decorative Tiles.

Regional Groups To find out if there is a branch of the Society near you, click on the map of United Kingdom or scroll down the page to browse through the list. This section also has regularly updated information on regional events.

Membership Help to save important buildings and learn about their past by becoming a member of the Society. Membership starts at £15 and entitles you to a thrice-yearly magazine. Click on the Membership Application Form at the bottom of the page, which you can print out and send off. There is also a place on the form for you to fill in your credit card details and subscribe online but, worryingly, this site does not appear to be secure.

OTHER FEATURES

If you want to see the most perfect example of a domestic, late-Victorian interior in the entire country, then click on Linley Sambourne House. The home to cartoonist and illustrator Edward Linley Sambourne from 1874 to 1946, it is an unrivalled evocation of the Aesthetic style. It is situated just off London's High Street Kensington, and the site gives details of its opening times. If you want to learn more about the Society's work, Saving Buildings gives a brief introduction. You can also email them from this page to volunteer your help or inform them of a threatened building.

An excellent site which slips in its grading due to the migraine-inducing tiny print.

OTHER SITES OF INTEREST

The Association of British Insurers
www.abi.org.uk
This site is most useful to the homeowner for its Consumer Advice and Information section. Many of their Information Sheets are stored in PDF format so that you can save them to your machine and view or print them later. The sheets are mercifully free of jargon and give sound, current, advice on motor, holiday, homes and contents, health, medical, and life insurance.

Breakglass
www.breakglass.co.uk
This site offers instant advice on home disasters although, by definition, you will probably want to read it in a quiet moment rather than waiting until the washing machine has flooded the hall or your child's fingers are hovering dangerously close to the electricity sockets. It offers straightforward advice in the First Aid, Gas, and Fire sections. Click on Emergency Solutions to Electrical and Plumbing Problems for stopgap fixes for water leaks and electrical problems.

Burgled.com
www.burgled.com
This is a practical site which manages to reassure its readers rather than filling them with terror. It guides those unfortunate enough to have been burgled through the gruelling aftermath and gives advice on how to prevent yourself from being broken into in the first place. Recently Been Burgled? offers details of organisations which provide services and support to victims of burglary. Making Your Home Safer gives a checklist of things you can do to make your home more secure without turning it into a fortress. How Safe is Your Neighbourhood? gives detailed information on every borough and district in England with links to specific councils for further information, too. At the

time of writing, the addition of Wales, Scotland, and Ireland to this section was imminent.

The Council of Mortgage Lenders
www.cml.org.uk

The site of this trade association contains much helpful information for the homeowner. Go to FAQs & Links for clear, succinct advice on the most common general queries of borrowers. These include sections on How to Buy A Home, How to Buy A Home in Scotland, You and Your Mortgage, Assistance with Mortgage Repayments, and Mortgage Calculator. It's not a site that is going to set the world alight with its beauty, but its sheer usefulness makes up for its lack of glamour.

The Geffrye Museum
www.geffrye-museum.org.uk

If you are interested in the history of the English domestic interior, this museum should most definitely be on your list of places to visit. Set in a row of Grade II Listed, Eighteenth Century almshouses in London's Shoreditch, it comprises a chronologically arranged series of rooms covering the seventeenth to the twentieth centuries. Look at the Events and Activities Calendar to learn about conferences, lectures, workshops for adults and children, and the special exhibitions they hold in their stunning modern extension. For the green-fingered, the gardens are also laid out in historically correct plots. Friends of the Museum can enjoy private views, guided walks, and visits to private collections – all for a minimum donation of £10.

Heritage
www.heritage.co.uk

Plunder this site for a wealth of information on owning and renovating old buildings. There are links to many useful organisations, but perhaps the most alluring is the intriguing, idiosyncratic Pavilions of Splendour, an ideal location for a half-an-hours' fantasy shopping. This award-winning site identifies buildings of architectural or historical importance which are for sale. At the time of writing, these included the birthplace of the Bronte sisters in Thornton, West Yorkshire, and also watertowers, almshouses, coach houses, a bakehouse, chapels, and London's smallest house, a sliver of elegant loveliness in Harrow-on-the-Hill. You can register your interest and receive updates if anything that matches your requirements comes on the market.

The Home Repossession Page
www.home-repo.org

Half a million homes have been repossessed in the past 10 years. If this has happened to you, or you think it is about to, this site offers compassionate, up-to-date advice, and sheds a little light on what has been, hitherto, a secret shame.

Journalist Lee Kimber set up the site in 1997 when his mortgage lender repossessed his flat and sold it for the princely sum of £5,600, leaving him with considerable arrears. Initially the aim of the site was to provide advice to those who felt their repossessed homes had been sold by their lender at well below market value and to support them in their right to question the sale without intimidation or legal threat. Today advice is offered to those who are just beginning to get into arrears too. There are listings for charities, organisations and websites which offer free advice, and information from others who have suffered at the hands of unscrupulous or unethical lenders.

HM Land Registry
www.landreg.gov.uk

If you ever wondered what the Land Registry does, then this is the place to find out. The site gives admirably jargon-free explanations of various aspects of the government organisation, including Publications & Forms which allows you to print off the documents you need for lodging applications. Property Prices provides information on average prices and sales volume of residential property across the country. Find the nearest of the 24 Regional

Offices to you by using the drop-down menu; when you find your local office, click search to obtain contact details. Fees provides an indication of the prices of registering or modifying an entry in the land register.

The Museum of Domestic Design & Architecture
www.moda.mdx.ac.uk

The Museum of Domestic Design and Architecture (MoDA) is part of the University of Middlesex, and contains one of the world's most comprehensive collections of decorative arts from the period 1870 to 1960. They have a fine collection of trade catalogues from furnishers and decorators, wallpapers, fabrics, and a very good library of books on design, architecture, and decoration. Their brand new building opened in October 2000 in Barnet; use the drop-down menu to find out about Exhibitions and Events, and Introduction to the Permanent Collection and Workshops. MODA by mail order offers a selection of CD-ROMs, catalogues, and books. Related Sites gives links to other decorative arts museums across the world.

CONTACTS LIST

And finally ... You can't buy online from all of these sites – indeed some are no more than a simple web presence to remind you of their existence – but they may be useful if you're in need of inspiration, or a list of contacts.

Bathrooms

www.alternative-plans.co.uk

www.astonmatthews.co.uk

www.bathaus.co.uk

www.bathroomsint.com

www.colourwash.co.uk

www.cphart.co.uk

www.designer-bathrooms.co.uk

www.duravit.com

www.gecanderson.co.uk

www.hansgrohe.co.uk (taps etc)

www.ideal-standard.co.uk

www.inda.net

www.kaldewei.de

www.maxpike.com

www.sissons.co.uk

www.svedbergs.co.uk

www.teuco.com

www.tsunami.interiors.co.uk

www.villeroy-boch.com

www.westonebathrooms.com

www.williamgarvey.co.uk

Kitchens

www.aeg.co.uk

www.alternative-plans.co.uk

www.amtico.com (flooring)

www.baumatic.com

www.blum.com

www.boschappliances.co.uk

www.bradshaw.co.uk

www.brandt.com

www.chalon.com

www.clivechristian.com

www.corian.com

www.cotteswood.co.uk

www.crabtreekitchens.co.uk

www.dadaweb.it

www.dedietrich.co.uk

www.hotpoint.co.uk

www.houseoffraser.co.uk

www.ikea.co.uk

www.indesite.com

www.kahrs.se

www.majesticcooker.co.uk

www.miele.co.uk

www.mwf.com

www.neff.co.uk

www.newcastlefurniture.com

www.purves.co.uk

www.rational.de

www.shaker.co.uk

www.siematic.co.uk

www.siemensappliances.co.uk

www.smallbone.co.uk

www.smeguk.com

www.snaidero.com

www.varennapoliform.it

www.viaduct.co.uk

www.wattsandwright.com

Bedrooms

www.andsotobed.com

www.conranshop.com

www.designersguild.com

www.dicointernational.com

www.foundat.co.uk

www.harrison.co.uk

www.interluebke.de

www.kbbmag.com

www.paintworks.co.uk

www.relyon.co.uk

www.silentnight.co.uk

www.slumberland.co.uk

www.waterbed.co.uk

Glossary of Internet Terms

Accelerators Add-on programs, which speed up browsing.

Acceptable Use Policy Terms and conditions of using the internet, usually set by organisations who wish to regulate an individual's use of the internet. For example, an employer might issue a ruling on the type of email which can be sent from an office.

Access Provider A company which provides access to the internet, usually via a dial-up account. Companies such as AOL and Dircon charge for this, although there are an increasing number of free services such as Freeserve, Lineone and Tesco.net. Also known as an Internet Service Provider.

Account A user's internet connection, with an Access/ Internet Service Provider which usually has to be paid for.

Acrobat Reader Small freely-available program, or web browser plug-in, which lets you view a Portable Document Format (PDF) file.

Across Lite Plug-in which allows you to complete crossword puzzles online.

Address Location name for an email or internet site, which is the online equivalent of a postal address. It is usually composed of a unique series of words and punctuation, such as *my.name@house.co.uk*. See also URL.

America Online (AOL) World's most heavily subscribed online service provider.

Animated GIF Low-grade animation technique which is used on websites.

ASCII Stands for American Standard Code for Information Interchange. It is a coding standard which all computers can recognise, ensuring that if a character is entered on one part of the internet, the same character will be seen elsewhere.

ASCII Art Art made of letters and other symbols. Made up of simple text, so it can be recognised by different computers.

ASDL Stands for Asynchronous Digital Subscriber Line, which is a high speed copper wire which will allow rapid transfer of information. Not widely in use at moment, though the government is pushing for its early introduction.

Attachment A file included with an email, which may be composed of text, graphics and sound. Attachments are encoded for transfer across the internet, and can be viewed in their original form by the recipient. An attachment is the equivalent of putting a photograph with a letter in the post.

Bookmark A function of the Netscape Navigator browser which allows you to save a link to your favourite sites, so that you can return straight there without re-entering the address. Favourites in Internet Explorer is the same thing.

BPS Abbreviation of Bits Per Second, which is a measure of the speed at which information is transferred or downloaded.

Broadband A type of data transfer medium (usually a cable or wire) which can carry several signals at the same time. Most existing data transfer media are narrowband, and can only carry one signal at a time.

Browse Common term for looking around the web. See also Surfing.

Browser A generic term for the software that allows users to move and look around the Web. Netscape Navigator and Internet Explorer are the ones that most people are familiar with, accounting for 97 per cent of web hits.

Bulletin Board Service A BBS is a computer with a telephone connection, which allows you direct contact to upload and download information and converse with other users, via the computer. It was the forerunner to the online services and virtual communities of today.

Cache A temporary storage space on the hard drive of your computer, which stores downloaded websites. When you return to a website, information is retrieved from the cache and displayed more rapidly. This information may not be the most recent version for sites which are frequently updated; you will need to reload the website address for these.

Chat Talking to other users on the web in real time, but with typed instead of spoken words. Special software such as ICQ or MIRC is required before you can chat.

Chat Room An internet channel which allows several people to type in their messages and talk to one another over the internet.

Clickstream The trail that you leave as you 'click' your way around the web.

Codec Any technology which can compress/decompress data, such as MPEG and MP3.

Content The material on a website that actually relates to the site, and is hopefully of interest or value. Things like adverts are not considered to be part of the content. The term is also used to refer to information on the internet that can be seen by users, as opposed to programming and other background information.

Cookie A cookie is a nugget of information sometimes sent by websites to your hard drive when you visit. They contain such details as what you looked at, what you ordered, and can add more information, so that the website can be customised to suit you.

Cybercafe Cafe where you can use a computer terminal to browse the net for a small fee.

Cyberspace When first coined by the sci-fi author William Gibson, it meant a shared hallucination which occured when people logged on to computer networks. Now, it refers to the virtual space you're in when on the internet.

Dial Up A temporary telephone connection to your ISP's computer and how you make contact with your ISP, each time you log onto the Internet.

Domain The part of an Internet address which identifies an individual computer, and can often be a business or person's name. For example, in the goodwebguide.com the domain name is theGoodWebGuide.

Download Transfer of information from an Internet server to your computer.

Dynamic HTML Most recent version of the HTML standard.

Ecash Electronic cash, used to make transactions on the internet.

Ecommerce The name for business which is carried out over the internet.

Email Mail delivered electronically over the internet. Usually comprised of text messages, but can contain illustrations, music and animations. Mail is sent to an email address: the internet equivalent of a postal address.

Encryption A process whereby information is scrambled to produce a 'coded message', so that it can't be read while in transit on the internet. The recipient must have decryption software in order to read the message.

Expire Term referring to newsgroup postings which are automatically deleted after a fixed period of time.

Ezine Publication on the web, which is updated regularly.

FAQ Stands for frequently asked questions and is a common section on websites where the most common enquiries and their answers are archived.

Frame A method which splits web pages into several windows.

FTP/File Transfer Protocol Standard method for transporting files across the internet.

GIF/Graphics Interchange Format A format in which graphics are compressed, and a popular method of putting images onto the internet, as they take little time to download.

Gopher Precursor of the world wide web, consisting of archives accessed via a menu and organised by subject.

GUI/Graphical User Interface. This is the system which turns binary information into the words and images format you can see on your computer screen. For example, instead of seeing the computer language which denotes the presence of your toolbar, you actually see a toolbar.

Hackers A term used to refer to expert programmers who used their skills to break into computer systems, just for the fun of it. Nowadays the word is more commonly associated with computer criminals, or Crackers.

Header Basic indication of what's in an email: who it's from, when it was sent, and what it's about.

Hit When a file is downloaded from a website it is referred to as a 'hit'. Measuring the number of hits is a rough method of counting how many people visit a website. Not wholly accurate as one website can contain many files, so one visit may generate several hits.

Homepage Usually associated with a personal site, but can also refer to the first page on your browser, or the first page of a website.

Host Computer on which a website is stored. A host computer may store several websites, and usually has a fast, powerful connection to the internet. Also known as a Server.

HTML/Hypertext Mark-Up Language The computer code used to construct web pages.

HTTP/Hypertext Transfer Protocol The protocol for moving HTML files across the web.

Hyperlink A word or graphic formatted so that when you click on it, you move from one area to another. See also hypertext.

Hypertext Text within a document, formatted so it acts as a link between pages, or from one document to another.

Image Map A graphic which contains hyperlinks.

Interface What you actually see on the computer screen.

Internet One or more computers connected to one another is an internet (lower case i). The Internet is the biggest of all the internets, consisting of a worldwide collection of interconnected computer networks.

Internet Explorer One of the most popular pieces of browser software, produced by Microsoft.

Intranet A network of computers which works in the same way as an internet but for internal use, such as within a corporation.

ISDN/Integrated Services Digital Network Digital telephone line which facilitates fast connections, transfers large amounts of data and can carry more than one form of data.

ISP/Internet Service Provider See Access Provider.

Java Programming language which can be used to create interactive multimedia effects on web pages. Used to create programmes known as *applets* that add features such as animations, sound and even games to websites.

Javascript A scripting language which, like Java, can be used to add extra multimedia features. However, it does not consist of separate programmes. Javascript is embedded into the HTML text and can interpreted by the browser, provided that the user has a javascript enabled browser.

JPEG Stands for 'Joint Photographic Experts Group' and is the name given to a type of format which compresses photos so that they can be seen on the web.

Kill file A function which allows a user to block incoming information from unwanted sources. Normally used on email and newsreaders.

LAN/Local Area Network A type of internet, but limited to a single area, such as an office.

Login The account name or password needed to access a computer system.

Link Connection between web pages, or between one web document and another, which are accessed via formatted text and graphic.

Mailing List A discussion group which is associated with a website. Participants send their emails to the site, and it is copied and sent by the server to other individuals on the mailing list.

Modem A device for converting digital data into analogue signals for transmission along standard phone lines. The usual way for home users to connect to the internet or log into their email accounts. May be internal (built into the computer) or external (a desk-top box connected to the computer).

MP3 A compressed music file format, which has almost no loss of quality although the compression rate may be very high.

Netscape Popular browser, now owned by AOL.

Newbie Term for someone new to the Internet. Used pejoratively of newcomers to bulletin boards or chat, who commit the sin of asking obvious questions or failing to observe the 'netiquette'.

Newsgroup Discussion group made up of Internet users who share an interest. There are thousands of newsgroups covering every possible subject.

Offline Not connected to the internet via a telephone line.

Online Connected to the internet via a telephone line.

Offline Browsing A function of the browser software, which allows the user to download pages and read them while they are offline.

Online Service Provider Similar to an access provider, but provides additional features such as live chat.

PDF/Portable Document Format A file format created by Adobe for offline reading of brochures, reports and other documents with complex graphic design. Can be read by anyone with Acrobat Reader.

Plug-in Piece of software which adds more functions (such as playing music or video) to another, larger software program.

POP3/Post Office Protocol An email protocol that allows you to pick up your mail from any location on the web.

Portal A website which offers many services, such as search engines, email and chat rooms, and to which people are likely to return to often. ISPs such as Yahoo and Alta Vista provide portal sites which are the first thing you see when you log on, and in theory act as gateways to the rest of the web.

Post/Posting Information sent to a usenet group, bulletin board, message board or by email.

PPP/Point to Point Protocol The agreed way of sending data over dial-up connections, so that the user's computer, the modem and the Internet Server can all recognise it. It is the protocol which allows you to get online.

Protocol Convention detailing a set of actions that computers in a network must follow so that they can understand one another.

Query Request for specific information from a database.

RAM /Random Access Memory Your computer's short-term memory.

Realplayer A plug-in program that allows you to view video in real-time and listen to sound and which is becoming increasingly important for web use.

Router A computer program which acts as an interface between two networks and decides how to route information.

Searchable Database A database on a website which allows the user to search for information, usually be keyword.

Search Engine Programs which enable web users to search for pages and sites using keywords. They are usually to be found on portal sites and browser homepages. Infoseek, Alta Vista and Lycos are some of the popular search engines.

Secure Transactions Information transfers which are encrypted so that only the sender and recipient have access to the uncoded message, so that the details within remain private. The term is most commonly used to refer to credit card transactions, although other information can be sent in a secure form.

Server A powerful computer that has a permanent fast connection to the internet. Such computers are usually owned by companies and act as host computers for websites.

Sign-on To connect to the internet and start using one of its facilities.

Shareware Software that doesn't have to be paid for or test version of software that the user can access for free, as a trial before buying it.

Skins Simple software that allows the user to change the appearance of an application.

Standard A style which the whole of the computer industry has agreed upon. Industry standards mean that hardware and software produced by the various different computer companies will work with one another.

Stream A technique for processing data, which enables it to be downloaded as a continuous stream, and viewed or listened to as the data arrives.

Surfing Slang for looking around the Internet, without any particular aim, following links from site to site.

TLA/Three Letter Acronyms Netspeak for the abbreviations of net jargon, such as BPS (Bits Per Second) and ISP (Internet Service Provider).

Upload To send files from your computer to another on the internet. When you send an email you are uploading a file.

URL/Uniform Resource Locator Jargon for an address on the internet, such as www.thegoodwebguide.co.uk.

Usenet A network of newsgroups, which form a worldwide system, on which anyone can post 'news'.

Virtual Community Name given to a congregation of regular mailing list/ newsgroup users.

VRML/Virtual Reality Modeling Language Method for creating 3D environments on the web.

Wallpaper Description of the sometimes hectic background patterns which appear behind the text on some websites.

Web Based Email/Webmail Email accounts such as Hotmail and Rocketmail, which are accessed via an Internet browser rather than an email program such as Outlook Express. Webmail has to be typed while the user is online, but can accessed from anywhere on the Web.

Webmaster A person responsible for a web server. May also be known as System Administrator.

Web Page Document that forms one part of a website (though some sites are a single page), usually formatted in HTML.

Web Ring Loose association of websites which are usually dedicated to the same subject and often contain links to one another.

Website A collection of related web pages which often belong to an individual or organisation and are about the same subject.

World Wide Web The part of the Internet which is easy to get around and see. The term is often mistakely interchanged with Internet, though the two are not the same. If the Internet is a shopping mall, with shops, depots, and delivery bays, then the web is the actual shops which the customers see and use.

Index

o8oo4homes.com 118
123 Sort-it 68
a2zcarpet 99
accessories;
  bathroom 32, 33, 40, 43, 64
  bedroom 32, 33, 40, 43, 55, 64, 65
  children's 33-35, 43, 45, 50, 52, 57, 59, 61, 64
  decorating 13, 17
  gifts 33-35, 50, 52, 54, 60-65, 114
  home furnishings 32-35, 38, 39, 41, 43, 44, 47, 50, 52, 53, 55, 57-65, 70, 114
  ordering products, see online ordering
  tableware 33, 52-55, 59, 60, 64, 65
  wedding accessories 33
  wedding gifts 33, 34
acrylics 45
address book, see shopping
Advanced Diploma in Interior Design, see courses
advice in your home;
  furnishings 46
  Feng Shui 113
Aesthetic style 125
Alba Tops 61
Alfie's Antique Market 86
AllAboutHome 96
All that Women Want 68
All the Right Moves 15
All Things Frugal 103
American House Beautiful 79
Ancient style furniture reproductions 61

Anderson, Robin 118
animals, see pets
Annie Sloan School of Decoration 109
anti-allergy bedding, see bedlinen
antiques, general 68, 71-73, 77, 79, 82-93, 128
  addresses 86, 87
  auctions 65, 68, 79, 84, 85, 91, 92
  care 68, 85, 88, 89
  china, glassware and pottery 72, 83, 84, 88
  children's 89
  courses, see courses
  dealers and experts 79, 83-85, 90
  fairs 71, 79, 83, 85
  guarantees 83
  ordering, see online ordering
  queries, see Frequently Asked Questions
  reclaimed items and materials 86, 89, 90, 92
  repair, restoration and conservation 37, 85, 87
  replicas and reproductions 61
  security 85
  silver 84
  valuations 84
Antiques at Antiqnet 91
antiques.co.uk 82
Antiques Roadshow 83, 84, 88, 89, 113
anti-slip matting 45
apartment, decorating a 73
appliances, see kitchen

equipment, sound and vision
Arad, Ron 64, 65
architects 76, 119
  see also, contractors
architectural salvage, see antiques (reclaimed materials)
architecture 75, 79, 119, 120, 121, 124, 125, 127, 128
archives, see magazine articles
Arcsal Architectural Antiques 86
armchairs, see chairs
arms and armour 82
arranging;
  flowers 72, 107
  furniture, see room schemes
arrears 127
art, see antiques, courses
Art Deco style furniture reproductions 61
Art Nouveau style furniture reproductions 61
Art Room 61
Arts & Crafts 41, 44
Associate Diploma in Interior Design, see courses
Association of British Insurers, the 126
Astor, Annabel 53
astrologers, see horoscopes
attics 112
auctions, see antiques

B&Q 16, 26
Bachelor of Arts degree in interior design, see courses
BAFRA, see British Antique

Furniture Restorers' Association
bags, see accessories (gifts)
Bakelite 91
Bamford, Trudie 70
barbeque, general 51
  ordering products, see online ordering
Barker, Godfrey 83
bars, see catering industry
baskets, see storage
bathrooms, general 19, 32, 36, 41, 43, 44, 63, 64, 75
  fittings 37, 63
  lighting 37
  linen 32, 34, 40, 41, 46, 47, 63, 64
  ordering products, see online ordering
  see also, antiques (reclaimed items)
Battie, David 88, 113
bay windows, see curtains
BBC Antiques Roadshow 83, 84
BBC Online Homes 14
BBC Online Antiques on the Web 88, 89, 103
beauty products 79, 98
bedding, see bedlinen
bedlinen, general 32, 34, 35, 36, 40, 41, 43, 44, 46, 47, 50, 59, 64
  ordering products, see online ordering
bedrooms 32, 34, 35, 43, 44, 55, 64, 65, 79
beds 39, 55, 63
bedspreads, see bedlinen

Beme.com 79
bespoke, see made-to-order
Better Homes & Gardens 69
blankets, see bedlinen
blinds 13, 44, 63, 120
BLUEdeco.com 54
Bly, John 83
Bonham's 91
booklets, see factsheets
books, see architecture,
cooking, courses
borrowing, see mortgages
breadmakers, see kitchen
equipment
Breakglass 126
bricklayers, see contractors
brickwork, Victorian 125
briefing, see contractors
brightbeige 70
British Antique Furniture
Restorers' Association 87, 88,
102
BRIX, see Builders' Resource
and Information Exchange
Brulé, Tyler 76
budget;
  bathroom linen and bedlinen
  46
  Christmas 102
  decorating 28, 78
  everything 103
  home care 98, 102
  weddings 73
builders, see contractors
Builders' Resource and
Information Exchange, the 123
building, general 123
  materials, see antiques
  (reclaimed materials)
  see also, architecture
burglary;
  prevention 96, 122, 126, 127
  victims 126, 127
Burgled.com 126, 127

buying;
  houses, see property
  see also, online ordering

CAB, the 15
calculation of paint quantity
required 12
Cambridge Fine Furnishings
110
Campbell, Nina 22, 41
candles, general 51, 62-64,
108
  ordering products, see online
  ordering
candlesticks, see accessories
(tableware)
cards, see greetings cards
carpenters, see contractors
carpets, see rugs
Carte du Jour 50
Casa 24
cast iron, see decorative
hardware
catalogues 128
catering industry;
  eating out locally 122
  interior design for 112, 113
ceramics, see antiques, china,
pottery
Certificate in Interior
Design/Decoration, see
courses
Chair Company, the 61
chairs 39, 44, 47, 54, 55, 58,
61, 62, 64, 65
chandeliers, see lighting
Changing Rooms 14
checks, see fabric, wallpaper
Chelsea Flower Show 107
chests of drawers, see
furniture
Chiasmus 62
children's goods, see
accessories, antiques,

furniture
china, general 33, 54, 55, 59,
62, 64, 65
  ordering products, see online
  ordering
  see also, antiques
Christie's 91, 114
Christmas 51, 69, 77, 78, 102,
107
  ordering products, see online
  ordering
ChristmasOrganizing 77
Christopher Wray Lighting 37
church architecture, see
antiques (reclaimed items)
Churchill, Jane 27
Citizens' Advice Bureau, the 15
City & Guilds, general 114
  Certificates in Interior Design
  112, 113
  Certificates in the History of
English Furniture 113
cleaning, see home
Click Deco 62
Codygifts 62
coins 85
collectibles, see antiques
collecting, see antiques
collections, replicas of pieces
  from 61
colleges near your home 122
colon cleansing 114
colour, general 12, 17, 24, 33
  consultancy service 22
  schemes 13, 17, 70, 113
colourwashing 74
combing, see paint (effects)
comics for collectors 91
competitions 64, 75, 79, 89
conservation;
  antiques 87, 88
  energy 96
  historic buildings 120, 121,
  124, 125, 127

Conservation Building
Products Limited 89
consultancy, see courses
(interior design)
consumer advice;
  decorating 13
  insurance 126
  property 15
Contemporary Living 62
Contemporary style furniture
reproductions 61
contractors;
  briefing 17, 20, 21
  contract 21, 26, 124
  employing 17, 20, 21, 45, 87,
  123
  guarantee of work 17, 20, 21,
  124
  queries, see Frequently Asked
Questions
  vetting 20, 21, 26
conversion;
  measurements 14
  articles into lamps 37
conveyancing 123
cooking;
  books 51
  equipment, see kitchen
equipment
  ingredients 51, 103
  ordering products, see online
ordering (kitchen equipment)
  recipes and techniques 61,
  68, 69, 71-73, 76, 77, 97, 98,
  100, 101
copies, see antiques (replicas
and reproductions)
Council of Mortgage Lenders,
  the 127
Country Life 79
Country Living 71, 79
Country Sampler Decorating
  Ideas Magazine 74
country style decorating 71, 74

courses;
antiques 88, 107, 113, 127
art and painting 107, 108, 112, 113
crafts 110, 111, 114, 115
Feng Shui 113
flower arranging 107, 108
furniture decoration and restoration 109, 115
historic buildings 120, 121, 125, 127
interior design 106-115, 128
needlework 47
soft furnishings and upholstery 110, 113, 115
coverage 12, 27
crafts, general 36, 46, 47, 69, 72-74, 77, 78, 98, 102, 110, 111
fairs 71
Crafts Council, the 42
creative arts, see courses
credit card security, see shopping
crime 122
Criterion Tiles 28
Crossland, Neisha 22
Crown Paints 12
crystal, see glassware
Cube Collection, the 55
Cucina Direct 60
curtains;
accessories and poles 37, 39, 41, 44, 46, 55, 59
bay windows 46, 59
buying secondhand 38
made-to-order 44, 46
ordering products, see online ordering
patterns 46
range 13, 14, 38, 41, 55, 59, 120
readymade 38, 39, 59
selling secondhand 38
Curtain Exchange, the 38

cushions, see accessories
cutlery, see accessories (tableware)

Damask 34
dealers, see antiques
Debbie Travis' Painted House 25
decorating, general 14, 15, 26, 28, 68-79, 101, 118, 124
ordering products, see online ordering
queries, see Frequently Asked Questions
Decorating Your Home 28
decorative arts;
societies 111
see also, antiques
decorative hardware, general 37, 46, 54, 63, 125
ordering products, see online ordering
see also, antiques (reclaimed items), door furniture
decorators, see contractors
Decorator Secrets 28
decoupage 25, 44, 74, 78
degree in interior design, see courses
demographics 122
demolition;
preventing, see conservation
reclaimed items and materials, see antiques
demonstrations, see courses
department stores 65
design;
shows 62
see also, accessories, courses, decorating, fabrics, furniture, interior design, etc.
designers, see interior designers
Designers Guild 33

Design Online 28
Dining Chair Company, the 62
dining room, see accessories, china, glassware, home furnishings, tables, tablelinen
Diploma in Interior Design, see courses
Direct Life & Pensions 123
dishes, see kitchen equipment
Divertimenti 55
DIY;
ordering products, see online ordering
products 13, 16, 17, 19, 29, 65, 69
projects 14, 16, 29
queries, see Frequently Asked Questions
techniques 14, 15, 29
DIYFixit 28
DIY SOS 14
doctors near your home 122
DoItYourself.com 29
domestic appliances, see kitchen equipment
door furniture, general 37, 46
ordering products, see online ordering
doors, general 29
see also, antiques (reclaimed items)
Dormy House, the 35
dried flowers 107
drink, see cooking, eating out, entertaining, wine
Dualit toasters 60
Dulux International 17
DuPont SmartPaint 26
duvets, see bedlinen

Eames, Charles and Ray 64
Easter 69
eating out 122
economy, see budget

education;
near your home 122
see also, courses
Edwardian architecture 125
electrical;
appliances, see kitchen equipment, sound and vision
problems 126
electricians, see contractors
electrics, see DIY products, lighting
energy efficiency 96
English Country House Style 107
English Heritage 88
English Stamp Company, the 18
entertaining, general 69, 71, 73, 76-78, 107
see also accessories (tableware), cooking (recipes)
environmentally friendly cleaning 98, 101
European style furniture reproductions 61
Europe by Net 62
Ewer, Cynthia Townley 97
exhibitions, see antiques (fairs), museums, stately homes

fabrics 13, 19, 33, 34, 41, 43, 44, 46, 47, 52
Fabric World 46
facilities near your home 122
factsheets and booklets;
architecture and historic buildings 120, 121, 125
crafts 69, 72
DIY and decorating 14, 16, 17, 69, 72
home care 97
fairs, see antiques
Fallon, Tricia 62

family 68, 79
fantasy browsing 84, 127
FAQs, see Frequently Asked
  Questions
Farrow & Ball 27
faux finishes 69
Federation of Master Builders
  123
Feng Shui;
  courses, see courses
  queries, see Frequently Asked
  Questions
Feng Shui Art of Space
  Clearing, the 113
finance, general 15, 21, 73, 118
  see also, grants, mortgages
fine art, see antiques
Finelot 83
Fired Earth 19
fireplaces, general 120
  see also, antiques (reclaimed
  items)
fire safety 96, 126
first aid 126
flat, decorating a 73
flea markets, see antiques
  (fairs)
flooring 14, 19
floorplans, see room schemes
floral;
  art 107, 108
  prints, see fabrics, wallpaper
flowers 60, 72, 107
flower shows 107
food, see cooking, eating out,
  entertaining
football club towels and
  bedlinen 47
Foundation Course Design
Certificate, see courses
fragrances 35, 114
freezer, see cooking (recipes)
Frequently Asked Questions/
  FAQs;

antiques 83
carpets and rugs 99
contractors 20, 26
decorating 13, 16, 25, 26, 28,
  70, 71, 74, 75, 115
DIY 16, 29
Feng Shui 114
home care 64, 77, 96
property and mortgages 118,
  127
stamping 18
furniture, general 33-35, 39,
  40, 44, 52-55, 58, 61-65
  children's 33, 34
  layout, see room schemes
  loose covers 44
  paint/upholster yourself 35,
  44
  ordering products, see online
  ordering
  replicas and reproductions
  61
  upholstery 44, 47, 118
  see also, antiques, beds,
  chairs, courses (interior
  design), home ottomans,
  room dividers, sofas, storage,
  tables
Furniture 123 62
further education near your
  home 122

gardening, general 36, 43, 51,
  64, 65, 68-73, 79, 102, 124,
  127
  ordering products, see online
  ordering
  see also, antiques (reclaimed
  items)
gas 126
gates, see antiques (reclaimed
  items)
GCSE results 122
Geddes-Brown, Leslie 64

Geffrye Museum, the 127
General Trading Company, the
  63
geometric prints, see fabrics,
  wallpaper
geopathic stress 114
Georgian Group, the 120
gifts, see accessories
gift wrapping 33, 64
gilding 109
giveaways, see competitions
glassware, general 33, 43, 54,
  55, 59, 62, 64, 65
  ordering products, see online
  ordering
glazes 27, 44, 45
glitter paint 22, 110
Good Housekeeping 79
Grafton, Christy 74
granite, see paint (effects)
grants for conservation and
  renovation 124
Grattan-Bellew, Sophie 22
greetings cards 62
guarantees, see antiques,
  contractors
guided tours, see museums,
  stately homes
guides to online home shopping,
  see shopping
Guild, Tricia 33
Guinevere Antiques Online 92

Habitat 39
Haf Designs 63
Hall, Alvin 15
Hambledon Gallery 58
Hampton Court Flower Show 107
Handbag.com 56
hardware, general 13
  see also, decorative hardware
Haslam, Nicholas 118
headboards, see bedrooms
health services near your

home 122
heating engineers, see
  contractors
Heloise 100
Hennessy, Noel 64
heritage, see conservation
Heritage.co.uk 127
Hilary's Blinds 63
Hilton, Matthew 65
Hints from Heloise 100
history 120, 121, 124, 125, 127
HM Land Registry 127
Holding Company, the 57
home;
  cleaning 60, 61, 72, 73, 77,
  88, 89, 96-103
  furnishings 13, 19, 32, 33, 35,
  36, 40, 43, 44, 46, 47, 50, 58,
  62-4, 124
  furnishings advice in your
  home 46
  history 118
  improvement 21, 28, 29, 69
  improvement loan 21
  maintenance 14, 68, 73, 79,
  124
  office 35, 51, 57, 63, 64, 65,
  79
  ordering furnishing products,
  see online ordering
  organization 57, 68, 97, 98,
  103
  problems 126
  queries, see Frequently Asked
  Questions
  small repairs 68
  see also, accessories,
  courses, decorating,
  Frequently Asked Questions,
  online advice, security
HomeArts 79
Homebase 13, 24
Home Dec in a Sec 46
HomeDecoratingSite 77

Home Elements Ltd 50
Home Front 15
Home Front Inside Out 15
HomePro.com 79
Home Repossession Page, the 127
Hoppen, Kelly 19
horoscopes 68, 84
hotels, see catering industry
House, see Hambledon Gallery
House Beautiful 75
household appliances, see kitchen equipment
HouseNet 36
houses, see property
housing, see property
housekeeping, see home
Hugh Scully's World of Antiques 84

ice-cream makers, see kitchen equipment
icollector.com 92
Impressionists style furniture reproductions 61
Improveline 21
Inchbald School of Design 111
Inhabit 63
inks 18
In-Sinks 63
instruction sheets, see factsheets
insurance;
  antiques 86
  health and medical 126
  holiday 126
  life 123, 126
  motor 126
  property 118, 123, 126
interior design 46, 63
  see also, courses
interior designers, general 20, 28, 62, 64, 65, 79, 118
  competitions 64

see also, contractors
Interior Design Information Service, the 28
Interior Internet 63
Intersaver 63
investment 15
Iron-Bed Company, the 63
ironwork, see decorative hardware

Jackson, Alison 62
Jim Lawrence Traditional Ironwork 37
John Lewis 63, 64
Jones, Sue 53
Just Doors 29

Kennedy, Peggy 75
Kenneth Turner Flower School 107, 108
kettles, see kitchen equipment
Kimber, Lee 127
Kitchen, John WL 88
kitchens;
  equipment 50, 51, 55, 60, 62-65, 77, 96
  fittings 37, 63
  ordering products, see online ordering
  planning layout 69, 75
  safety 96
  worksurfaces 61
  see also, antiques (reclaimed items)
kit houses 118
Kingston, Karen 113
kitsch 62, 63
KLC School 106
knives, see kitchen equipment
knitting, see crafts
Knobs & Knockers 46
Kode 64
Kyoto 53

Ladies' Home Journal Online 79
Lakeland Limited, 51
lamps & lampshades, see lighting
Land Registry 127
LAPADA 85, 103
LASSCO 92
laundry, see storage
Lawrence, Jim 37
Law-Turner, Dr Freddie 82
layout of furniture, see room schemes
leaflets, see factsheets
Learn2.com 68
learning, see courses
legal advice;
  property 118
  see also, contractors
leisure 122
lenders, see mortgages
Leslie Geddes-Brown's Online Shopping and Mail Order Made Easy 64
letting, see property
Liberty 41, 64
life assurance 123, 126
lighting, general 14, 36, 37, 59, 62, 64
  accessories and fittings 37, 44, 63
  antique 37, 86
  ordering products, see online ordering
  repair and restoration service 37
  see also, antiques (reclaimed items)
linen, see bathroom linen, bedroom linen, tablelinen
Linens-Online 46
Linley Sambourne, Edward 126
Linley Sambourne House 126
Little, Antony 41

Living 78
living room, see accessories, chairs, home furnishings, sofas, tables
loans;
  conservation and renovation 124
  see also, mortgages
local authorities 124
local facilities and services 122
loft rooms 112
London Guildhall University 109
loose covers, see courses (soft furnishings and upholstery), furniture

made-to-order;
  blinds 63
  curtains 44, 46
  dining chairs 62
  flower arrangements 108
  home furnishings 47
  kitchen worksurfaces 61
  pottery 50
  rugs 47
Maelstrom 64
magazine articles;
  antiques 83, 88, 93
  decorating and DIY 16, 70, 71, 74-76, 78
  gardening 16, 71
  home care 98
makeovers, see decorating, interior design, room schemes
markets, general 65
  see also, antiques (fairs)
Marks & Spencer 40
Martha Stewart Online 72
MasterBond Warranty Scheme 124
master builders 123
Master of Arts degree in

Interior Decoration, see courses
mattress protectors, see bedlinen
McCalls decorating patterns 46
McCloud, Kevin 19
McCord Online 52
MDF 35, 36, 44
menus, see entertaining, cooking (recipes)
metallic paint 12, 22
metalwork, see decorative hardware
Miller, Judith 92
millinery 111
mirrors, using 77
mixing paint 12, 24
MoDA, see Museum of Domestic Design & Architecture
money saving, see budget
Morley-Fletcher, Hugo 83
Morris & Co 44
Morris, Helen 23
Morris, William 44, 121
mortgages, general 15, 21, 118, 122, 127
queries, see Frequently Asked Questions
mouldings 125
moving, see property
Museum of Domestic Design & Architecture, the 128
museums, general 88, 111, 120, 125, 127, 128
replicas of pieces 61
music 120

National Extension College 112
National Trust, the 88
needlepoint 47
needlework classes, see courses
neighbours 118
New Homemaker, the 103
Next 59

nightclothes 35
Noel Hennessy Furniture 64
Nono 47
Notley 63
nursery, see accessories, furniture

Oates, Roger 42
Ocean 64
ODLQC, see Open and Distance Learning Quality Council
Office of Fair Trading, the 15
offices;
   interior design 113
   see also, home (office)
OKA Direct 53
Oliver, David 22
online advice;
   decorating and DIY 16, 70, 72, 75
   garden 64
   gifts 65
   home care 64
   home shopping 64
   sewing for the home 36
online ordering;
   antiques 82
   barbeque 51
   bathroom linen 32, 40, 63, 64
   bedlinen 32, 40, 50, 52, 59, 64
   candles 51, 62, 64
   children's 33, 50, 52, 57, 59, 61, 64
   china 33, 54, 59, 62, 64, 65
   Christmas 51, 52
   curtains 40, 41, 59
   decorating products 22, 24, 27, 110
   DIY products and tools 13, 14, 20, 29
   door furniture and decorative hardware 46, 54, 63
   electrical appliances 63
   furniture 33, 40, 52, 54, 57,

61-65
   garden equipment 51
   gifts 33, 50, 54, 59, 60, 62, 64, 65
   glassware 33, 54, 59, 62, 64, 65
   home accessories 50, 52, 53, 59, 61, 64, 65
   home furnishings 32, 33, 40, 52, 53, 61, 64
   kitchen equipment and fittings 50, 51, 62, 63, 65
   lighting 37, 38, 40, 59, 62, 64
   rugs 41, 45, 59, 64
   stamping products 18
   stencilling products 23
   storage 51, 57, 60
   tablelinen 33, 64
   tableware accessories 33, 53, 59, 64
   weddings 33
online security, see shopping
online shopping, see shopping
online shopping list 16, 17
online wedding list 33, 65
Open and Distance Learning Quality Council, the 108
open house, see stately homes
organization, see home
Organizedhome.com 97
Osborne & Little 41
Osborne, Peter 41
ottomans 35

paint;
   acrylics 45
   calculating quantity 12
   coverage 12, 27
   effects and finishes 17, 24, 45, 109, 112, 113
   glitter 22, 110
   metallic 12, 22
   mixing 12, 24
   ordering, see online ordering

pearlescent 22, 110
   range of colour and type 12, 19, 22, 24, 26, 27, 43, 44, 45, 110, 120
   suitability for specific surfaces 13, 17, 27
   textured 12
Paint & Paper Library 22
painters, see contractors
painting;
   method and techniques 13, 24, 44, 45
   preparation 13, 24, 26
   service 36
Palumbo, Lady 47
pamphlets, see factsheets
pans, see kitchen equipment
paper, see wallpaper
parenting, see family
pastels 24, 33
patterns for home decorating 46, 69, 72
pawning valuable items 93
pearlescent paint 22, 110
pensions 123
perfumes, see fragrances
pets 53, 73
Phillips 92
photograph albums and frames, see accessories (gifts)
pigments, see paint
pillowcases, see bedlinen
pillows, see bedlinen
Pinnacle 21
Pioneerthinking.com 101
planning;
   life, see home (organization)
   room layout, see room schemes
plants encyclopaedia 72
plasterers, see contractors
Plexiglas furniture 55
plumbers, see contractors
plumbing 15, 16, 28, 126
porcelain, see antiques, china

postcode 122, 123, 126
pots, see kitchen equipment
pottery, general 50, 56, 65
  made-to-order 50
  see also, antiques
Practical Style 109
preparation, see painting
prints, see fabrics, wallpaper
problems, see Frequently
  Asked Questions
professionals, see contractors
property;
  buying 15, 21, 79, 118, 122-
  124, 127
  renting 15, 21, 70, 118, 122-
  124
  queries, see Frequently Asked
  Questions
  selling 13, 15, 96, 118, 122-124
  see also, mortgages, security
prospectus, see courses
protection, see conservation
Purves & Purves 65
queries & questions, see
  Frequently Asked Questions
quilting, see crafts
quilts, see bedlinen
quizzes, see competitions

radiators, see antiques
  (reclaimed items)
ragging, see paint (effects)
Rayner, Alan and Dorothy 51
rebirthing 114
recipes, see cooking
reclaimed materials, see
  antiques
Regent Academy 112
Reject Tile Shop, the 28
renovation;
  furniture, see antiques
  historic buildings 120, 121,
  124, 125, 127
  home, see decorating, DIY

renting houses, see property
repair and restoration, see
  antiques, renovation
repairs of items in the home,
  see home
replicas and reproductions,
  see antiques
repossession 127
restaurants, see catering
  industry
restoration, see antiques,
  renovation
retail therapy, see shopping
revamps, see decorating,
  interior design, room schemes
RHODEC International 108
RIBA, see Royal Institute of
  British Architects
Rocha, John 118
Roger Oates Design 42
roofers, see contractors
room dimensions 12, 13, 79
room dividers, general 35, 57, 74
  ordering products, see online
  ordering (furniture)
room schemes 17, 26, 46, 47,
  69, 76, 79, 113, 115
Royal Doulton 63, 65
Royal Institute of British
  Architects, the 119
Rug Company, the 47
rugs, general 19, 41-43, 45, 47,
  59, 64, 99
  care and cleaning of carpets
  and rugs 98, 99
  made-to-order 47
  making your own 78
  ordering products, see online
  ordering
  queries, see Frequently Asked
  Questions
  runners, see rugs

Sabatier knives 55

safety, see security
salvage, see antiques
  (reclaimed materials)
SalvoWEB 90
sample boards, see courses
  (interior design)
samples;
  decorating 17, 19, 22, 27, 46
  see also, swatches
Sandall, Thomas 76
Sanderson 43
SAVE 124
Save Britain's Heritage 124
saving;
  energy 96
  money, see budget
  water 96
scaffolders, see contractors
scents, see fragrances
schools near your home 122
Scotland, property in 127
screening, see contractors
screens, see room dividers
Screwfix Direct 29
Scully, Hugh 84
Scumble Goosie 44
security;
  antiques 85
  home 96, 122, 126
  online 56, 113
selling houses, see property
seminars, see courses
ServiceMaster 96
services near your home 122
sewing for the home, see
  crafts
Shafer, Tricia 78
Sharp, Christopher 47
Sheffield School of Interior
  Design 115
Shepherd, Wendy 102
Sheppard, Hilda 47
shopping;
  addresses 64, 65, 70, 79, 86

Handbag.com 56
Leslie Geddes-Brown 64
local shops 122
security of online shopping
  56, 113
Stylesource 65
surveys of online home
  shopping 56, 64, 70, 79, 102,
  118
TimeOut.com 65
  see also, online ordering
shower curtains, see bathrooms
shows, see television
  programmes
silks, see fabrics
silver, see antiques
Simple Living 101 98
sinks, see kitchen fittings
sitting room, see accessories,
  chairs, home furnishings,
  sofas, tables
SKK pots and pans 55
Small Island Trader 65
SmartPaint 26
Smeg 63
Smith, Delia 51, 55
Society for the Protection of
  Ancient Buildings, the 121
sofas, general 33, 39, 55, 58,
  64, 65
  ordering products, see online
  ordering (furniture)
soft furnishings, see home
  furnishings
Sotheby's 92, 93, 113, 114
sound and vision appliances
  63
  ordering products, see online
  ordering (electrical appliances)
SPAB, see Society for the
  Protection of Ancient Buildings
Space Clearing 113
Spectrum Paint 43, 44
Spittles, David 20

Spode 65
sports facilities near your home 122
stain removal, general 99-101 see also home (cleaning)
stair rods, see decorative hardware
stamp duty 123
stamping, general 18
ordering products, see online ordering
queries, see Frequently Asked Questions
Stanford Hall 110
Starck, Philippe 64, 65
stately homes 88, 120, 125
stationery, see accessories (gifts)
statistics 122
Stencil Library, the 23
stencilling, general 23
ordering products, see online ordering
Stewart, Martha 72, 77
stippling, see paint (effects)
stonework 120
storage, general 39, 51, 57, 58, 60
ordering products, see online ordering
stripes, see fabric, wallpaper
Stuart 65
student accommodation 118
study, see courses
STYLE-revolution 79
Stylesource 65
Suite101.com 73
surveys, see shopping
swatches 17, 22, 34, 35, 39, 43, 46, 47, 62, 63

tablelinen, general 33, 64
ordering products, see online ordering
tables, general 33, 35, 39, 54,

55, 58, 61, 64, 65
ordering products, see online ordering (furniture)
tableware, see accessories, china, glassware
Tapisserie 47
taps, see bathroom, kitchen fittings
tassels 110
television programmes;
antiques 71, 83, 84, 88, 89
decorating 13, 14, 25
templates, see patterns
textiles, see fabrics
textured paint 12
theft of antiques 91
This is Furniture 65
throws, see bedlinen
tiles 19, 28, 125
timber kit houses 118
TimeOut.com 65
Tipztime 102
toasters, see kitchen equipment
Todhunter, Emily 22, 34
tools, see DIY products
tortoiseshell, see paint (effects)
tours, see museums, stately homes
towels, see bathroom linen
toys, see accessories (children's) antiques
trade catalogues 128
tradespeople, see contractors
traditional materials and skills, see conservation
training, see courses
travel 62
Travis, Debbie 25
trays, see accessories (tableware)
Turner, Ken 107, 108

unemployment 122
University of Wales 111

upholstery, see courses, (furniture)
UpMyStreet.com 122
utilities near your home 122

valances, see bedlinen
valuations, see antiques, property
varnishes 45
vases, see accessories (home furnishings)
vetting, see contractors
Victoria & Albert Museum 19, 42, 88
Victoria magazine 79
Victorian Society, the 125
Victorian;
architecture 125
furniture reproductions 61
vision, see sound and vision appliances
visits, see museums, stately homes

Wallflowers' Home Decorating Projects and Ideas 47
wallpaper 22, 27, 33, 34, 41, 43, 44, 47, 120
Wallpaper.com 76
wallpapering 16
Walter, Dawna 57
warranty, see contractors (guarantee)
waste disposal units, see kitchen fittings
Watchdog 15
water;
filters, see kitchen fittings
saving 96
Waterford 65
Waterhouse, Lucinda 53
weather forecast 16
Weaver, Genevieve 92
weaves, see fabrics

Web Rugs 45
weddings, see accessories, budget, flowers, online ordering, online wedding list
Wedgwood 65
White Company, the 32
Willis, David 86
windowbox.com 73
windows 120
wine 76
wood 19, 44, 54
woodwash 12
woodwork 15
work, see family
work experience 107
working from home, see home (office)
workmen, see contractors
workshops, see courses
worksurfaces, for kitchens 61
workwomen, see contractors
World of Interiors Design Studio, the 47
Wray, Christopher 37
Wriglesworth, John 118
wrought iron, see decorative hardware
Wynn, Graham 79

Your Mortgage 122

Home and Interiors at the Good Web Guide

www.thegoodwebguide.co.uk

The good Web Guide site provides simple, one-click access to all the sites mentioned in this book, and is an easy way to start exploring the internet. All books about the internet become slightly out of date as soon as they're printed, but with the free updates you'll receive as a member of the GWG Parents Channel, this book will remain current for as long as you are member. Subscription to the channel usually costs £10 for a year, but by registering your purchase of this book you'll receive free membership for 6 months.

Navigate to the channel by typing in the address given above. You arrive at the main GWG homepage, which lists headlines for and links to some of the newest articles, reviews and competitions on the site, and details of special offers on other Good Web Guide books. To reach the Home Channel, click on the Home and Interiors button from the list of channels on the left-hand side of the page.

SPECIAL FEATURES

Registration Although some reviews and articles are free to view, the majority of content on the GWG site is accessible only to members. Begin by clicking on the small Register Now icon near the top left of the page. When you've filled in and submitted your details a menu will appear on the left of the page. Choose the option Register a Book Purchase. From the questions that appear, just type in the answer to the Home question (you'll need to have this book in front of you to find the answer) and your membership will give you instant access to all parts of the Home Channel. When you return to the site you will just have to log in with your user name and password to get your full privileges.

Home and Interiors Homepage provides a quick digest of the latest reviews and features. The full menu of sections within the channel appears on the left.

Website reviews You'll find the latest versions of all the reviews in this book, organised by chapter, together with new reviews in the Latest Additions section. At the bottom of each review there is a link straight to the site, so you don't need to worry about typing in the addresses. New reviews are added at least monthly, and sometimes weekly.

Search provides the simplest way of navigating the content on this site. The box appears at the top of every page and allows you to search either just within the Home and Interiors channel or the whole GWG site.

Features You'll find regularly updated articles here on best buys, new trends, renovating your home and up and coming designers.

Bookshelf If you need offline inspiration, you'll find reviews of the most up to date and mouthwatering books on design and home maintenance.

Offers A range of exclusive discounts for GWG members.

Newsletters Click on the Free Newsletters button to register for the monthly Home and Interiors email newsletter, or for as many GWG newsletters on other subjects as you wish.

Channels You can view a regularly changing selection of website reviews and articles from the other GWG channels. These include Gardening, Wine, Food, Health, Money, Home and Interiors, Travel, and Genealogy, with further channels in development.

As well as providing an up-to-date gateway to the top-quality home and interiors websites, this is a site to return to regularly for news and inspiration.

other great titles in thegoodwebguide series:

hardback £12.99

genealogy.......................... ISBN 1-903282-06-3
health.............................. ISBN 1-903282-08-x
home .... ISBN 1-903282-15-2
money............................. ISBN 1-903282-26-8
museums and galleries....... ISBN 1-903282-14-4
travel.............................. ISBN 1-903282-05-5
wine............................... ISBN 1-903282-04-7

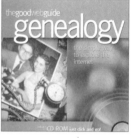

paperback £7.99

food .... ISBN 1-903282-17-9
gardening........................ ISBN 1-903282-16-0
parents........................... ISBN 1-903282-19-5

small paperbacks £4.99

comedy .... ISBN 1-903282-20-9
games............................. ISBN 1-903282-10-1
gay life............................ ISBN 1-903282-13-6
music............................. ISBN 1-903282-11-x
sex................................ ISBN 1-903282-09-8
sport .... ISBN 1-903282-07-1
tv .... ISBN 1-903282-12-8